100 Years

100 Years

Nancy Beckham Capra

100 Years
At the Spring Gap Ranch
© 2026 by Nancy Beckham Capra
Printed in the USA
All rights reserved.

Unless otherwise noted, all photos are courtesy the Beckham and Capra families.

Scripture taken from the New King James Version®. Copyright © 1982 by Thomas Nelson. Used by permission. All rights reserved.

Cover and Interior Design by Nancy Capra
Printed in the United States of America.
First Edition: April 14, 2026
ISBN: 979-8-9956990-0-2
Hardaway Beckham Publishing
For more information, visit: www.nancycapra.com

Soli Deo Gloria

In His hand are the deep places of the earth;
The heights of the hills are His also.
The sea is His, for He made it;
And His hands formed the dry land.
Psalm 95:4-5

THE HISTORY OF THE SPRING GAP RANCH is the history of names. For many years it was called the Beckham Ranch when my father, Bob Beckham, was the sole owner. Our parents were excellent stewards and very prayerful in all their endeavors. Long before they passed away, they gave the ranch to my siblings, John, Lynn, Rob Beckham and me. We still run it as a cow-calf operation and have eagerly anticipated its 100-year anniversary as a family ranch. 2026 is our centennial. We are considered a "Texas Family Land Heritage" ranch for running a continuous agricultural operation within the family. It honors the commitment and endurance of our relatives and our desire to pass down this legacy.

The ranch's final name change reflects and represents its unique location, the Spring Gap. It is an ode to a place of peace, endurance, and grit. As a family, we feel called to make it better and cultivate hope for future ranchers. It is a place to seek a good and right connection with the natural world. It is a story in tune with the earth and with the melody of the hills. But it is also a tale of drought, heatwave, and failures. My intention is to leave written documentation for future generations that they might encounter God and see His hand on their lives. In creating these pages, I asked my siblings, their spouses, and all our adult children to send me their thoughts and memories.

This is a family memoir, with different voices from different generations. Each story matters and gives a colorful snapshot of ranch life. We all long for Eden, for paradise. It's buried deep in every human heart but there is a struggle on this side of heaven and the ranch is my fallen Eden. It is teeming with briars, brambles, cactus, and manure. The redemptive side is also there in the flight of a red-tail hawk, the spots of the spring fawn, and a cow with a newborn calf. These chapters speak of the highs and the lows. How in every season God is faithful. He loves us. He cares for us. He will not leave or forsake us so we can walk forward knowing we are held. The pages continue to turn as our family has kept and cared for the Spring Gap Ranch. The way we've lived is perhaps a chance to see how our faith has guided us and also give new bearings for the way future generations will sustain this legacy.

Spring Gap Ranch
Land Succession

Godly Generations

**C.M. Caldwell pointing parade instructions as
Bob and Caldwell Beckham look on.**

ON EARTH AS IT IS IN HEAVEN

For the Lord is good; His mercy is everlasting,
And His truth endures to all generations.
Psalm 100:5

MY GREAT GRANDFATHER, Clifton Mott "C.M." Caldwell, had a boyhood ambition... become a lawyer, save his money and invest it. When he had 640 acres of land and 50 bald faced cattle, he was going to retire and become a rancher. In the same era, Richard Cordwent also had a boyhood dream of coming to America and building a vast land and cattle empire. It is doubtful the two men ever met, but the similarities in their character and vision make the story of the Spring Gap Ranch even more inspired. "Dick" Cordwent, as he was called by his friends, was born in England, educated and wealthy. His family did not share his love of adventure and disowned him. He and a cousin set sail for America. After exploring the northern states, they moved south to Texas and began running a small sheep herd on the open range. Dick started purchasing land and increasing his herd due to the shift from the open range to fenced lands. He did this all on his own without the help of his family.

C.M. also started with very little. He married Cora Keathly and said that she owned seven cows and he owned seven cows and she owned a horse and he had a buggy. It was a match made with heaven's blessing. This is probably the one difference between the two men that may have caused Dick to die at an early age. He was unmarried.

Dick Cordwent put the Cross Bar Ranch together in 1880. The illustrious ranch spread over 50,000 acres in the Spring Gap area in Callahan County. He was a bachelor. He was very British and very polite. Dick was a hard worker and brought himself up from an open range sheep herder to owning an empire of land, cattle, horses, sheep, and goats. He built 14 homes on the ranch for his hired help called String Town and paid his hands a dollar a day. He gave each family a milk cow. He made jobs for the people. When a school was needed for the children of the area, he volunteered to pay for it alone. Turkey Creek School cost him two thousand dollars. Dick made a lot of money by leasing land to oil companies. An oil well was dug on Cross Bar Ranch, but it was a dry hole.

C.M. and Cora worked hard for C.M. to become a lawyer. From the fruit of their labor, they helped make Breckenridge, Texas a civil and livable community. Much of their fortune was also made in oil. The Caldwells, like Dick Cordwent, were generous and faithful with their finances.

Bob Beckham, C.M.'s grandson and my dad, wrote a paper for his Elementary English class in 1946. In it he states, "In 1922, C.M. Caldwell moved his family to the neighboring town of Abilene to make it possible for his three children to attend college. He invested the money he had been able to make and save in ranches in the western part of Texas and in good cattle. Thus he has continued through the years to work with his cattle on his farm and ranches and enjoys doing so as well as any man living."

In 1924, Dick Cordwent died of a heart attack in West Texas in the Van Horn section of Culbertson County while loading cattle. He died without a will, so his brothers and sisters inherited his estate. To sell it, they had to communicate across the Atlantic Ocean and from South Africa to Britain. It is their names that are on the deed of sale filed April 14, 1926 to C.M. Caldwell.

C.M. purchased about 20 percent of the Cross Bar Ranch for a little over eight dollars an acre. He called it the Cordwent Ranch on documents speaking of cattle deals, tank cleanings, grass leases, fence building, and cedar chopping. He saw his land, cattle, and oil properties grow many times over his boyhood dreams. Cora and he were dedicated members at First Baptist Church in Abilene, Texas. They were quick to give to many projects in the community including donating the land that the original Hendrick Hospital sits on. Now he was considered a pretty good cowman.

Much of the heritage and history of the Spring Gap began as settlers seeking a better life migrated to the grasslands of West Texas. Many folks were moving to Callahan County from the east during the mid to late 1800's. Texas would give them 160 acres to homestead and farm the land. The days were numbered for the open range as fences crossed the prairie and family farming and ranching operations began to emerge. A man named Uncle George lived in a tent at the Uncle George well, thus that pasture was named in his honor. George Richardson lived at the Richardson windmill, another pasture that still carries his name—the Richardson. There were 32 sharecroppers at one time on the ranch because, back before the boll weevil, cotton was king. There is a story of a wagon train that was burned out somewhere in the Sneed pasture. A settler named Jim Malbee tried to ride off with an Indian Chief's daughter at the Turkey Creek School. These landmarks are long gone and they barely capture the hardships the homesteaders endured. They were small-time dirt farmers with big families and big problems making a living. There are ruins of numerous old homesteads all over the ranch. Lewis Nordyke chronicles those early days with clarity that touches all the senses. Here is a small excerpt from his book, Nubbin Ridge;

> Not only did we have soil under our fingernails and often be-
> hind the ear, we had it in our lungs and in the very blood in our
> veins. Everything we had came from the land—the fields, the
> garden, the woods, the hills. We lived by the will of nature. And
> by knowing some of her secrets, we sometimes tried to bend
> the will of nature. The sound of the wind in the trees, or moan-
> ing around the corner of the house or a cut in the hills, the
> complaining of the windmill, the blueness of the sky, the tex-
> ture of the clouds, the way the sun looked in the evening, the
> hue of the haze on the distant hills, the way the world smelled
> when we stepped outside and sniffed the breeze at dawn, the
> way the birds and animals acted, even the way a dog howled
> in the dead of night—-all these things meant something to us.
> (Nordyke 202)

It was in this environment that C.M. Caldwell purchased the ranch, and over the years, transferred it to his children, Guy, Mildred, and Agnes. They worked together to eventually trade pieces of land so that the parcel in Callahan County became the Beckham Ranch owned fully by my dad, Guy Robert Beckham, known as "Bob". A degree in animal husbandry at Texas Tech set Bob on his way to make ranching his life work, much to the delight of his parents, uncle, aunt, and grandfather. In 1956, Bob married Peggy Hardaway Patillo and four towheaded moppets of the 1960s started calling him Dad.

* * *

One of the sweetest stories was told to me by my brother, John Beck-ham, and recounts when our grandmother, Agnes Beckham, turned 70. She told Dad she wanted to ride a horse one more time. Dad took her to the ranch and saddled up Robin and another horse. Then they took a ride around the Horse pasture. Dad said she looked quite comfortable in the saddle. She had not forgotten her ranching past or her Hardin-Simmons white horse days! The beauty in this story is the godly and honoring way Dad treated his mother. One of his life credos was to stay humble—everyone is important and we should learn to relate to those that are different from us. Dad was admired, respected and considered a friend by all our foremen, bulldozer operators, fence builders, cowboys, cattle buyers, and neighbors. He was equally at home at a Bank Directors meeting as he was working cattle in the pens.

Austin Beckham, my nephew, put it this way, "I won't ever think about the ranch without thinking about Grandad. Watching him with people stuck with me. It didn't matter who you were — cowboy, foreman, doctor, rancher, or family — he treated everyone the same. People always wanted to talk to him, and he always made time. He was serious when he needed to be, but he was always laughing and making others laugh."

Emily Beckham Wood, my niece, remembers him this way, "Grandad modeled how to keep faith and family at the center of his life, how to find humor in every situation, and how to truly see and care for those around you. He taught me the power of companionship when sitting next to each other on a slow fishing day. He taught me how to work hard and not shy away from trying new things through working roundups. He played a central role in developing my love of animals, horseback riding, and dogs—even naming one of his own dogs after me (for the record, I was tickled about this!!!)."

Dad stewarded well the legacy he had been given. He saw people, places, and things as entrusted to his care. He found God in ordinary places through ordinary people. And he practiced what C.M. and even Dick Cordwent had done years earlier—he shared the land. So it is no surprise that Dad transferred ownership to my siblings and me while he was still able to run it. The name had already shifted from the Beckham Ranch to the Spring Gap Ranch. His capacity to serve and mentor others was a strong part of his character. Many boy scouts have camped at the Spring Gap. Field Trips of horticulture classes from local universities have identified plants. And deer hunts have been held with organizations serving youth. The Spring Gap was considered a Rehab Ranch and known for donating to the Roundup for Rehab Cattle Sale. This auction continues today with ranchers, buyers, and community members supporting the life-changing services provided by West Texas Rehabilitation Center. We are followers of the Jesus way, which means we offer hospitality. Often staff from the West Texas Rehab would travel to the ranch during cattle round ups to be a part of those heritage days, and to enjoy the country cooking offered after the work was done. Like C.M., Dad had become a pretty good cowman. In each act of stewardship, these inspiring relatives who shaped the land generations ago reflect the image of God.

* * *

The ranch has another legacy which only those raised in the country might understand. It is the tradition of early driving. To get to the Spring Gap one spends about half of the drive on the interstate highway. There might be a quick stop in Baird for a ham sandwich, but otherwise it is about 30 minutes from downtown Abilene to the FM 2228 turn off. That highway is etched deeply in my brain and the landmarks now overlap as my years of driving it have increased. It's funny how a stretch of road can hold so much anticipation. Once off the highway, Dad would pull to the side and swap seats with me. It didn't start that way, but once my legs had grown to reach the pedals, I was expected to handle both the wheel, gas, and brakes. It was often a bit unnerving as Dad was usually in a hurry to get to the foreman's house before he finished lunch. However, we never drove that road without him warning me to slow down for the train tracks and check both ways because, "sometimes that train guard might not be working." About half way on this part of the trek to the ranch, we veer to the right and onto a caliche base road that on hot summer days spits dust like a mad bull. This is the place we would change drivers if one of my siblings happened to be along.

Once on the dirt road, tales of nostalgia start to shake loose, and I hear about early settlers. We pass the once lively grocery store now covered in trumpet vines and falling in on itself. My radar goes up as the Spring Gap comes closer and I slow to make the very sharp left, then right, then curving a ways to the other side of the gap. Many times when the road is wet it becomes quite slick. This section is especially tricky. It seems to grow more narrow through the gap, and if a car is coming towards you, it often is not seen until the curve opens to it. So between sliding off the road or the surprising appearance of another vehicle, I spend a great deal of time overthinking this part of the drive. On the other side of the gap, I feel released because now we are on the ranch. There are places on the drive my heart looks forward to. The Red Tank gate that leads to the Edgar tank. The straight away section where many a stampede started. And finally, the fence line our trapper used to hang coyotes on to show Dad what he had accomplished and to claim his bounty. This is the final signal for a hard left turn. Then down through the butterfly bottom where many years later, my daughter, Twig Capra, and I marveled at the monarchs as they migrated south for the winter. Next a hard right, and finally a turn into ranch headquarters. Putting Dad's truck in park with both of us alive and breathing always felt like a great victory. As I became a licensed driver, Dad appreciated the company on the drive down, but on the way home he was snoring five minutes in. Somehow, he knew when to open his eyes and recognize Dairy Queen and a late afternoon snack. In asking my family for their memories there were several that are worth sharing.

Donald Capra, my son, remembers, "Grandad influenced me in so many ways I couldn't list them all. But with regards to the ranch, I always think about driving to it. Grandad knew the roads to the ranch even if he were blindfolded in a dust storm. He always drove with a speed that would make others nervous. As a child I loved the jostling and G-force and it made me think Grandad couldn't wait to be on the land. Grandad often would let us "drive" in his lap, and I don't believe he slowed much for our benefit."

Dr. Rob Beckham, my nephew, wrote, "One memory that immediately comes to mind is riding with him in Old Blue, his hunting-rigged pickup truck. As a young boy I think he could not hear my high-pitched voice but he used it as a teaching opportunity and taught me that it is respectful to look a man in the eyes as you have a conversation with them. I think this also helped him read my lips easier."

It wasn't just Dad who liked to "drive" the ranch. This came from Wade Caldwell, referring to my great uncle, who sold his part of the ranch to my dad. "I traveled with Guy several times and we drove his Ford Bronco pickup up one of the steep hills. I thought we were going to roll off and down the hill. I was about 13 and he was letting me drive." And even Rob, not to be confused with my nephew, Dr. Rob, had this scenario offered by his son, Austin, "My favorite memories are with my dad when I was between the ages of five and ten. We went to the ranch constantly. He would drive from Abilene until we hit the county road, and then it was my turn to drive. I was five years old, steering the wheel while he worked the gas. Sometimes we'd prank my brother, Alex, by going pretty fast while I "drove." Alex didn't like it."

Many roads have crossed the ranch. There are still areas on the ranch where the old farming terraces are visible. If you look past the ruins, you will find portraits of Godly people who shaped this place in the past. You will discover what these places reveal about the costs and rewards of following God who delights in places as well as people. The tapestry is woven here with threads of blood and sweat, barbed wire and feed sacks, fishing line and hiking boots. It is a place tended to with family care—on earth and from heaven.

Two

Guiding or Groaning

The next generation at the spring.

WHAT GOD CREATED

I will lift up my eyes to the hills—from whence comes my help?
My help comes from the Lord, who made heaven and earth.
Psalm 121:1-2

THERE IS A SANCTUARY that is not marked by a building or decorative sculptures. It is a place of deeply rooted peace. Lynn Beckham, my sister, met Jesus in the hushed and unrushed space of the natural spring. This is the wildest part of the Spring Gap Ranch. It begins with a pass between Spring Mesa and Bald Eagle Hill in east central Callahan County. Turkey Creek rises just south of Spring Mesa. It never fails to invite my eyes to move across the wide vista of the Spring Gap, two rocky, cedar-covered hills in a line of bluffs and canyons. The two tallest peaks in the Callahan Divide butt up against each other to create a beautiful place. Between the hills is a constricted winding gap barely wide enough for one car. Beside the road is a sometimes gurgling creek which is fed by the springs at the foot of the hills. The road winds for more than a mile between cliff bluffs and piles of rock, and is cut by deep ravines densely covered with cedars and oaks. It can feel moody. It is a place of constant subtle changes.

Emily Beckham Wood, who is a geologist, wrote the following description. The Spring Gap Ranch sits on some of the most impressive geology of Callahan County. The ranch is composed by predominantly two Cretaceous aged units, the Anters Formation (~145-100 million years old [M.a.], sandstones, conglomerates, and shales, mostly seen on the lower slopes and in the pastures and valleys) and the Edwards Limestone (~120-110 M.a., forming the fossil rich bluffs and caprocks). Additionally, the ranch hosts Neogene (23-2.6 M.a.) and Quaternary (2.6 M.a.- present) aged soils and alluvium resting on top of and cutting through the older rocks forming the rolling pastures and creek beds. There are some outcroppings of older Permian aged mudstones of the Admiral Formation (~300-250 M.a.) within Callahan County, however the dominant rocks are of the younger units described above.

The geomorphology of the 'ridge forming' Edwards Limestone, the 'slope and pasture forming' Antlers Formation, as well as the Neogene and Quaternary soils and creek bed deposits, are the very foundation of the Spring Gap Ranch. The 'gap' which Spring Gap Ranch was named from is a break in the Edwards Limestone capped ridgeline, with a natural spring exposed along the slope that transitions into the more sandstone/shale rich Antlers formation.

The paleoenvironment (ancient environment) of the Antlers Formation and the Edwards Limestone can be described as shoreline-shallow ocean, with the Anters Formation containing more of your beachfront/coastal environments (i.e. river delta deposits, sand, clay) and the Edwards Limestone representing a shallow ocean that was once teeming with life (i.e. LOTS of sea critter fossils can be found along these limestone ridges). The transition in time and rock type between the older Antlers Formation and the relatively younger Edwards Limestone represent a local rise in sea level thus flooding the once beach front property of the Antlers Formation to deposit the Edwards Limestone on top. Obviously, there is no longer a sea anywhere close to the Spring Gap Ranch, so to get to what we see today the sea level subsided and the rocks were then exposed to erosion and weathering, leaving behind the ridges and flatlands of the ranch today only covered over with Neogene-modern soils and alluvium.

Common fossils found mostly in the Edwards Limestone are large ammonites, sea urchins, bivalves, and gastropods. Additionally, both the Edwards Limestone and the Antlers Formation contain chert nodules (i.e. silica deposits within the rock), which provided the material needed for the Native Americans to carve the many arrow heads that can be found at the ranch.

* * *

Whoever has felt the longing in nature, who yearns to reconnect, who values the special relationships with family and friends will love the Spring Gap. It is a true place of earthly beauty and soaring hope. There are stories of settlers using the spring as a watering stop as they traveled. These individuals were of strong faith and courageous character. This was also a favorite picnic spot for the homesteaders. Many end of school celebrations, Sunday school classes, 4th of July parties, and Saturday night stunts were held in this dark cool stretch of creation.

One of the most interesting stories involved Donald. He was a tactical flight officer for the Amarillo Police Department working with the Texas Department of Public Safety Aircraft Division helicopter out of Amarillo. Early on a Sunday, he was called to the hanger for a possible domestic violence where the female party had wandered off. As the pilot and he were making preparations to fly the helicopter and aid the search, something rang a bell for him. He plugged the coordinates into Google Earth and then told the pilot that the woman was on our ranch. They called the trooper in Callahan County to confirm the location and Donald shared more about geographic features of the Spring Gap. In fact she had been down in the spring where many unofficial parties and campfires were held. Luckily, she was found rather quickly with the added information of the area. She was unharmed and the helicopter was not needed.

The Gap can be a gateway to the world. Or an escape from it. My nephew, Robert Davis, remembers that every trip to the ranch ended with a stop to the spring located right off the county road. He knew if there had been some rain it would be a magical place. Our family allowed the sharing of the spring for many years. It was appreciated by locals as a special place. As the years went by and liability grew, it became the job of the ranch foreman to investigate any visitors. Later, that too became dangerous, and we finally painted the fence poles purple, which in Texas means no trespassing. The question became are we God's helpers or the reason creation groans? Damage to the landscape and the unique natural formations had to be protected. It is easier to keep wilderness areas than to create them.

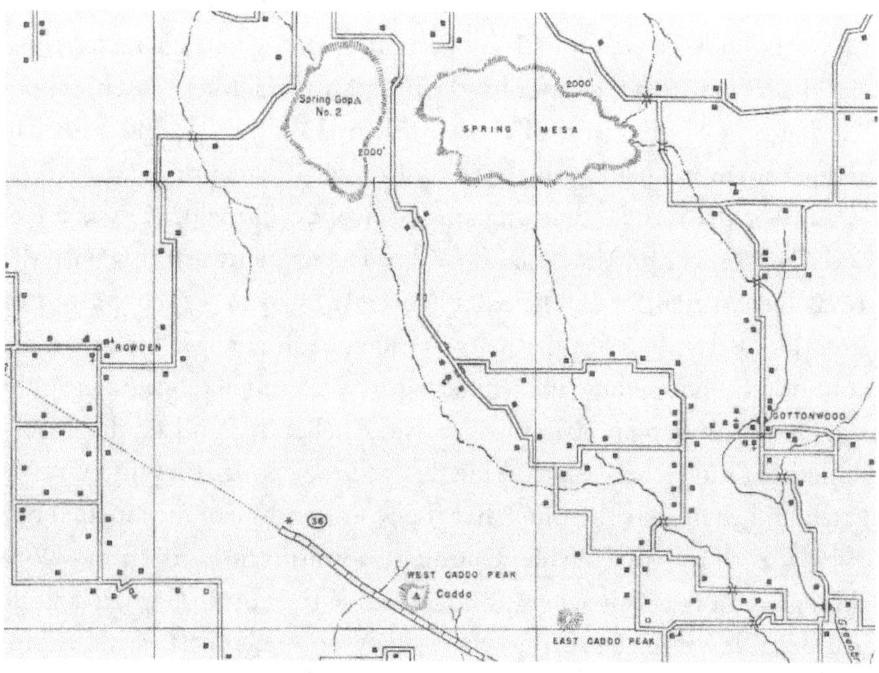

Callahan County

Sibling Partners

Three

Pastures and Preparation

Bob Beckham and Pete Ware

THE LIFE OF THE FOREMAN

Trust in the Lord with all your heart,
And lean not on your own understanding;
In all your ways acknowledge Him,
And He shall direct your paths.
Proverbs 3:5-6

THE FOREMAN OF OUR RANCH is adept in many trades. The job entails running and maintaining the ranch and a cow/calf operation on 10,000 acres. We currently run from 150 to 180 good commercial Angus cows and approximately nine registered Angus bulls. Calves are usually sold after weaning, but sometimes are held over winter as yearlings. Besides knowing and working cattle, other desired skills include experience operating a bulldozer and grader for road maintenance, fence repair, basic mechanic skills, and water well repair/plumbing. Living on the ranch is required. This is not an easy life but it is deeply desired by a chosen few. On the Spring Gap we have had five foreman over the 100 years. Cecil Goble was the son of Dick Cordwent's foreman, Richard Goble. The family knew the land well and continued to assist C.M. with cattle and fences. Not much has survived in documenting those days except for a few letters mentioning deals and instructions.

> I remember Vernon's red hair!
> wrote my cousin Scott Palmer.

And everything that is said pertaining to temper and that bright crimson hair was manifested in this foreman of my childhood. In the 1960s people were not as socially aware as they are today. Vernon's drinking and abuse would have been grounds for termination. John shares the following biographies of the four Spring Gap Ranch foreman that we have known and worked beside.

Vernon Heatly was old school and felt anything worth doing needed to be done from horseback. He did not care much for fixing fences, working on water troughs or keeping things tidy around the headquarters. When I first started going to the ranch in third grade, I lived the first two summers in his guest room. His wife, Audrey, was a great cook... of anything fried! My job consisted often of being put out on a fence with a sack lunch, a roll of bailing wire and my pliers, and I would go down the fence line as far as I could tying up and patching holes in the fence. Vernon would then pick me up at the end of the day. Vernon did not care for company, and was not a good manager of people. One July day, when I was 15 and Rob was 10, he had us riding around in the pickup checking on cattle in the morning, when it was cool, and then after lunch, when it was over 100°, had us shoveling oats out of the oat bin. We should have done the reverse. It nearly killed us! Dad let Vernon go shortly after that episode.

Pete Ware was foreman for my high school and college days and was a great foreman and friend. He taught me much on fixing things, fence work, and cattle. His wife was Joyce, and they had four daughters that caused some drama from time to time. Pete's best friend was Smoky Callaway, Rodney Callaway's father. Both have been invaluable cowboys at our roundups. Pete died of cancer in the mid 1990's.

Tommy Rogers was a true Renaissance man. He was a gifted artist, avid reader, cow whisperer, horse (and donkey) trainer, trapper, philosopher, electrician, plumber, history buff, and general jack of all trades. He enjoyed company while working and was much fun to be around. Tommy and his wife, Susie, made a great pair and had a good influence on my children, Michael, Rob and Emily. Tommy was foreman from 1994 until 2015 and his tenure corresponded with our kids growing up years. They each spent a good portion of several summers working at the ranch under Tommy and Susie's guidance.

Alfredo Rodriquez is a great representation of the American dream. He was born and grew up in La Luz, Mexico. As a teenager, he swam the Rio Grande each spring and summer season and came to Texas for work. At some point, he got into the cowboy line of work eventually becoming a foreman for the Gibson Ranch near Brownwood. Many of these years were working under a green card, but Mr. Gibson encouraged him to study and obtain his citizenship. He and his wife, Angelica, both studied, passed their tests and received their US citizenship. However, Alfredo did have some personality quirks and had a way of creating drama. He was set to retire at the end of June 2026, but unexpectedly walked off the job two months early leaving the new foreman, Jerome Hargus, and the family with a challenge. God is good all the time and it made for an intense and sweet time of working together.

Vernon, Pete, Tommy, and Alfredo were all unique in their own way. Dad had a way of hiring good, authentic people and treating them fairly. Pete's daughter, Rhonda, wrote a letter to my dad after he passed that says it best. He always thought of you as one of his best friends. The love he felt for you was more like a brother than a friend. He spent the happiest years of his life working on your ranch...Daddy spoke often of you being the best boss a man ever had.

John spoke earlier of the influence Tommy Rogers had on his children. They came up with the term **Tommyisms** and here are a few from their memories. To an outsider, he might not be considered a scholar, with his broad sweat stained hat and leathered hands. But it only takes a short time in his presence to realize that he is a philosopher at heart and is remarkably well read, his favorite author being Mark Twain. After high school, ranching became his way of life.

Michael Beckham shares that to express surprise about a rattlesnake under a barrel they flipped over (in a very calm and unsurprised voice, while he meanwhile is jumping backwards): "**Well if that don't beat a goose gobblin'**." To express pleasure at his wife's delicious cake: "Now

Susie, **that'd make a jackrabbit spit in the eye of a bulldog!"** To explain why he needed a nap:

1. **"I'm gonna go think up some answers, in case somebody asks me some questions later."**

2. **"I'm gonna go examine my eyelids for holes that need patching."**

And from Chelsea Beckham: I had never been on a ranch before, let alone working on a ranch. I showed up to spend the weekend with my future husband's family having no idea what I was getting myself into. We woke up early and met Tommy at a broken windmill. I was a bright-eyed 19-year-old willing to help. At this point in my life, I had no idea how a windmill worked, but as you can guess I was about to find out. Tommy, somewhere along the line, decided I would be a good person to drive "Old Blue" to help fix this windmill. "Old Blue" was a sacred ranch truck loved by all. My job was to back up or drive forward on Tommy's hand motions to raise and lower the sucker rods which were hooked up to a pulley. I was terrified I would back up too much or move too far forward. I had never even driven a truck. But there I was, behind the wheel by myself acting like I knew what I was doing. Thankfully, I didn't ruin the ranch or even mess up the windmill. It was then I was called one of the best compliments I have ever received. After knowing Tommy for only hours, he called me a **"tough little outfit"**. It was a day I will never forget. Emily Beckham Wood remembers that Tommy and Susie introduced her to **'fried mush'**, a small loaf of cornmeal soaked in bacon grease kept in their freezer that they would slice off and fry from time to time...so good! "I see that now even in the busyness of my everyday life, deep friendships are worth the time invested. When I put on the scuffed up red boots and spurs that Tommy gave me, the quiet of the country calls to me and I am reminded of the blessing that he has been in my life."

* * *

Running a ranch takes a distinct type of person. They have country roots and country ethics. They are salt of the earth people of great kindness, honesty, and dependability. They invite you in for tea and ask how your family is doing. They are willing to help if you get stuck, or to advise you where they saw a big deer or a bunch of pigs. From cigarette smoke to homemade tortillas, we've needed them all. The ranch foreman is weighed down by thoughts of every task that needs attention. He is firmly grounded in the needs of the day, with one eye on the weather and the other watching over freshly dropped calves.

The Spring Gap Ranch denotes a place of survival. It is a name. It is a life force. The health of it relies heavily on the foreman. His ability to notice even the slightest details is necessary, especially as cows are calving and sometimes need assistance. It is also a place of spiritual pilgrimage where we can be quiet and contemplative. A location to lay a quilt and dream as the clouds pass by. Creation is good and we are made to enjoy it. It is a landscape where beauty has been created, and as rain and wind and time pass, it gets created again and again. We tend our hearts here in this place God has entrusted to us.

Bob Beckham and Tommy Rogers

Four

Cowboys, Cattle, and Chaos

Bob Beckham

A GOOD AND TERRIBLE STORY

For every beast of the forest is Mine,
And the cattle on a thousand hills.
Psalm 50:10

"WAKE UP! WAKE UP! We gotta get a move on." roars my dad.

The moon had not even thought of setting and it would be hours before sunrise. My body rolled out of bed already in my jeans and work shirt so all I had to do was pull on my boots. No hairbrush would touch my already pony tailed locks and a baseball cap could go a long way to cover this lack of hygiene. I quickly brushed my teeth and out the door we went. Usually I grabbed a Pop-Tart because I knew it was a long way to lunch. Living in town and not on the ranch had some drawbacks. In the truck I tried to sit with the ability to slouch against the door and perhaps get a few extra winks in. But since this was not the fun driving lesson experience on normal work days, I bounced and jostled most of the way allowing no sleep. We still slowed down for the train crossing, and then I'm pretty sure we flew over it. The adrenaline was pumping for my dad and all my siblings. I was an oddball in the family. I was not crazy about horses and riding without an adult nearby. And the cattle scared me. My bad attitude cwas birthed on those crazy dark morning drives. But thankfully we were made to participate. Life on the ranch moved according to the seasonal rhythms. We have two roundups each year, spring and fall. A cattle roundup is the essential, traditional process of gathering livestock from fenced pastures into a central location for branding, health management, and transport. As soon as we pulled into headquarters, it was everybody piling out at once to grab a bridle, catch and saddle the horses. But I needed a reset before the fast and furious began. This is where I paused for the smell. Whether spring or fall, each had a unique wafting essence. It was a bouquet of broomweed mixed with morning dew and horse. It was saddle leather and juniper. It only took one whiff and it changed the atmosphere. That bad attitude got kicked to the curb and joking with the cowboys began. There have been several men and a few women who have worked for us. The main and most continual crew during my lifetime were the Baize brothers, Paige and Arlon, Paige's son, Donny Baize, Sammy Cochran, and Rodney Callaway. Lynn and I judged everyone by looks and we were sure one of us would marry Arlon. He however, has remained a bachelor, and the rumor is there are still many single ladies in Baird cooking meals for him. Those men were the frame around my security during roundups. They watched over us, spring and fall, like a hen with chicks and never complained. They knew we were setting down roots at the ranch and nurtured us to love this life. The ranch shapes the spirit, keeps the spirit. The ranch shapes time, keeps time.

* * *

Rob wrote the following piece so that his grandchildren would have a testimony of an event that formed him deeply, like a brand on a calf never to be lost.

Many of my guiding values were shaped from the days we worked the cattle. Dad had a crew of day-work cowboys that he had spent years forming up. By the time I was a participant, the crew was an all-star group of true cowboys. These men worked on big ranches all over the state of Texas, trailering their horse and saddle wherever the next job was.

I remember Dad would wake us up well before daylight and we would scramble around getting ready and throwing down whatever

Mom had gotten together for breakfast and piling into Dad's Suburban for the 45-minute drive from Abilene to the ranch. I always loved that it was an excused absence from school!

The cowboys were already there and saddled but it was still pitch black. I was usually anxious because it made me feel like we were slowing things down. I would bounce out and run to the tack shed and grab my reins to catch my horse, usually Lax or Double A. The pen was pretty good sized and sometimes presented a challenge to catch a horse that had not been ridden in six months, but sometimes with help from Arlon or Paige, I would get the job done. Back at the tack shed, I would grab my saddle and pull off any dirtdobber nests that had been built in between roundups. After all of us were saddled and mounted, we would take off at a steady trot to the pasture we were gathering.

It was a surreal experience, my butt slapping between air and saddle because my legs weren't long enough to squeeze the horse, listening to Arlon talk about a horse he was training and watching Donny lope up ahead to the gate so we all could just ride through. It was kind of a contest to see who could get to the gate first to open it, a way of showing respect to the other riders.

In order to gather a pasture, the plan was for all of us to ride to the back corner, Dad would usually put the least experienced rider, me, in the corner. My job was simple, ride along the fence and stay even with everybody else as we moved towards the pens. The crew would ride along the back fence spreading out evenly until the last cowboy got to the other corner of the pasture. That cowboy, usually Paige or Arlon, would let out a whoop, signaling all of us to begin hollering and moving in unison. Dad was smart about spreading the "good" cowboys in between the learners. On one such occasion, Paige and I were waiting in the corner for the signal, the sun was just beginning the crest over the horizon, there was a little fog settled into the creek bottom below, the grass was a lush green and you could hear the crows beginning to stir. There was a chill in the air and I was just taking it all in when Paige dropped some cowboy wisdom on me. He said, "The best picture frame in the world is that space between your horses' ears." At that moment, I understood the peace and joy of a daywork cowboy. The respect for God's creation, the joy of appreciating the view, and the partnership between man and horse.

Gathering a pasture was organized chaos! You could ride the whole way to the end without seeing any cattle, thinking you were messing up or you might start and immediately encounter 20 head not wanting to cooperate. You were constantly trying to maintain a line but you rarely could see the other riders. Your yelling, whooping, and whistling served two purposes. One to get the cattle moving, the other to let the other riders know your location. You are alone, you have a set responsibility, and if you encounter cattle, it's on you to make sure they get to headquarters. Looking back on it, I realize the experience imparted confidence to take on challenges, to embrace uncertainty, to know the benefits of teamwork and the beauty of the present.

* * *

The cowboys are mighty men, well trained and established. Paige Baize comes from a family of godly parents and talented siblings. His brother, Wayne, is an acclaimed western painter, and Arlon lives at home taking care of their aging parents. Paige married and had children. He worked all over the state, and when the rodeo was in town, we knew we would see Arlon, Donny, and him working the alley and keeping riders safe. They weren't wealthy by man's standard but had everything they needed and were content. Many of their cowboying escapades are written in Paige's book titled, Remembering. The following is an excerpt from his chapter called Bob Beckham's Gathering.

We were going to have to gather that old Richardson pasture. It is a hard pasture to gather. I can't remember who all was working. I know there was Truett Davis, Raymond Dickson, Buddy Smith, Bob Beckham, and me and I can't remember if Arlon was there or not. That old Richardson pasture is a rough big ole pasture and that was before they ever pushed it and burned it. It is up and down and hard to gather and the pens sat right up on top of the hill. That was the only pens that they had then. You had to go up on the ridge right up on that backbone and pen right there at those pens. If I remember right there was about one hundred and twenty-five cows in there. About half of them were Brangus cows that were pretty trotty and the others were some old Angus cows that were kind of spoiled. They would run a little ways then stop and lay down. At night we would take what we had penned up there and drive them to headquarters and put them in a trap.

We thought we lacked three cows. It was a cloudy day and drizzling rain. It had been that way all week. I was riding a little horse of Bob's. It was one of his day working horses named Button. Me and old Button were down in the bottom over there and we hit those three cows. Boy, they just took off as hard as they could. I get turned around pretty easy and I didn't realize I was turned around. Those cows were running north, but I thought we were going south. I was really riding hard, trying to get ahead of them and it seemed like every time I would get to where I could head them, we would have to cross a canyon or draw or something. They would get back ahead of me again. I was fighting as hard as I could, finally we were coming up toward that backbone. I thought that as soon as I get to that backbone, I'll get right there and turn them. Maybe the others would have heard me and we could go right down that backbone to the pens. Just as we climbed out on top there on that backbone, I got to the front to turn them, but there the pens were. I was going the right way the whole time and didn't know it. They just ran behind that wing and ran in the pens. Of course nobody knew that it was an accident except me. I stepped down and closed the gate.

There was a man coming to me and he said, "I believe that was the prettiest job of cowboying that I have ever seen." I told

> him "Thank you." I didn't bother to tell him that I was trying to head them off instead of pen them. (Baize 72 -73)

Once back at headquarters cattle are sorted and "worked". This is a dangerous time because they are already stirred up from the gathering. We are a praying family. Sometimes we have prayed out loud in the morning before starting the roundup. Sometimes it is silent and personal out on the horse. But we are always asking God to watch over us on these days. On this roundup I wasn't there, but this is my recollection of what happened. The steer was particularly mad. Dad was as infuriated as the steer and wrapped his arms around its neck. The steer dropped his head then hurled it upward. Dad bent over the steer just in time to receive the full force of his skull against Dad's sinuses. The steer bounded away, bucking, twisting and whirling and never looking back. Dad told the cowboys to keep working and he went and laid down under some oak trees. He didn't look good and ended up in the hospital with smashed sinuses and a lot to think about. Those days of wild west roundups have settled down. Here is how John explains it.

> There have been lots of changes over the years, but perhaps the greatest is in the way we do roundup. We used to do it the old-style cowboy way. Round up used to be three to four day events, with 15 cowboys on horseback. We would gather 300+ cows with their calves and 250 or so yearlings. The cattle were wild and would throw their tails up in the air and start running when they saw you coming. You never got them all, happy if you got 90 percent. The yearlings we would usually keep in the Red Tank pasture since it was the largest at nearly 2000 acres and the roughest with much elevation change. We would come out of the bottoms at a full run, and hope to keep them together to reach the gate in the corner out onto the county road. Usually, it would take two or three tries – and you would have to wait at least a day or two between attempts to let the cattle calm down. I can think

of one horse that broke its leg (and had to be shot) gathering the year-lings. In order to not have to push the cattle too far, we built work-ing pens in the large pastures of the ranch – the Sneed, Uncle George, Richardson, Blue Tank, and the main pens at the headquarters.

Today, we don't use any horses, do all our work at the headquar-ters pens, and we are usually finished in the middle of the afternoon on the first day. Now, we run 150 to 180 mother cows and sometimes keep 100 yearlings. Starting with Tommy Rogers, we relied on the ranch pick-up with a feed bin and cattle that have been conditioned to come for feed when they hear the siren. When needed, we use four-wheelers, rather than horses. The cattle are much more gentle. We can work with six cowboys, rather than 14 or 15. I'm thankful that I got to experience the wild days, but the way we do it today is much more efficient and less dangerous.

* * *

Love of horses runs deep, and Lynn has it in her blood. As mentioned earlier, I'm not drawn to the ride, and the last time I worked on horse-back I could barely walk the next day. The thing about our work horses is that they aren't ridden much between roundups. And horses are al-ways "fresh" in the early morning meaning they are ready to rodeo. So while it is common to expect a little pushback from below the saddle the rider is expecting and alert to it. Being retired from riding, my job was to use a RTV vehicle to help block the road so the cattle could get to the pens safely. Lynn was still riding a horse. She had walked him in circles and done some other rider stuff to get his hiccups worked out. The sun was just beginning to light the day. It was about time for the horses to head out and Lynn's steed did a little side step that she was not ready for. It caused her to be separated from the saddle and she wound up on the ground. But it wasn't a normal fall. The way she landed caused her to injure her shoulder so bad she was in tremendous pain. She had to go to the hospital immediately, a good hour away. Logically, I was the one to take her so the roundup could continue. I have never prayed so hard and driven so fast in my life. My hazard lights were on and I hoped we would get there quickly. Lynn's pain was verbal and my heart ached for her. It was my worst day at the ranch and I wasn't the injured one. It turned out she had broken her arm and she healed over time. Lynn still loves horses and rides on occasion. Her grit and passion continue to shape the opportunities she has given her children and grandchildren.

* * *

Dad experimented with different breeds of cattle to find the best suited for our ranch's topography – Herford, Brangus, Limousine, and finally Black Angus. He raised us to not get attached to the young calves as they would soon be gone. To some it might seem harsh, but we knew that our cattle were providing nutrition and life to others. Dad always took excellent care of the livestock and he taught us to respect the gift of raising cattle. He challenged us to make our vocations, our avocations. It becomes a meaningful work of our minds, hearts and hands. Donald has a unique perspective on the shifting generations as we work the herd.

Roundup has always been special because it brings the people involved together. Family I might not have seen recently, the cowboys, the foreman, and others all come together to work the cows. Because of the uniqueness of this event, often there are others who just come to observe. It is these times I reflect on how blessed I am to be a part of this "work" not work. As time has flowed, the purpose and use for the ranch hasn't changed very much. As Grandad's legacy was passed down, the business and heart of the ranch hasn't shifted away from producing beef. However, as my generation has grown up working cattle roundups, I have seen the change in where folks stand relative to the branding iron. My aunt and uncles are now worrying about the rainfall totals, cattle prices, and the pregnancy rates. The big picture items. My cousins and I are now the ones able to handle the flipping tables and chutes, the shots and the calf pushing. Now my children, nieces and nephews get to begin cautiously helping and learning, not just where burgers come from, but how much effort and care goes into the ranch and allows it to succeed.

Arlon Baize and Sammy Cochran

Arlon Branding

Ear clipping day.

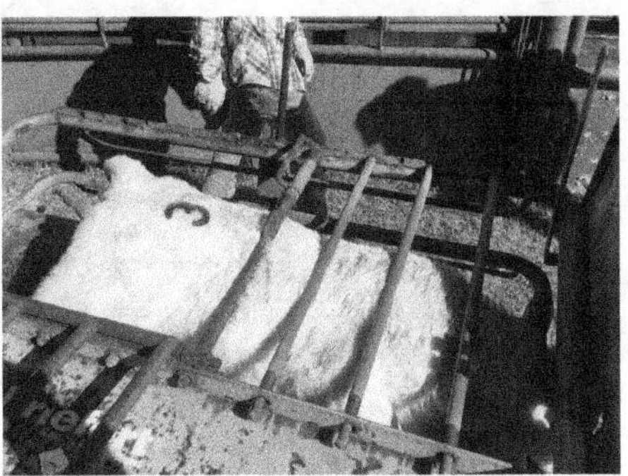

Lazy Three Brand

Five

Tasty Traditions

Mid-morning Snickers Candy Bar

AN EXCUSE TO GATHER

One generation shall praise Your works to another,
And shall declare Your mighty acts.
Psalm 145:4

HOW DO WE FILL our shared spaces with love? At the Spring Gap Ranch it's with food. When roundups occur you can be sure that Rob will have a carton of Snickers candy bars ready to hand out mid-morning. Even before that there have been homemade tortillas filled with egg, bean, and chorizo for breakfast tacos. The work is hard and stomachs empty fast burning those calories as they dodge cows and wrangle calves. There is always a cooler filled with drinks right next to the working table in the pens. It's quite an upgrade from my childhood when we had the Coleman jug filled by water from the hose with a community tin cup wired to the handle. We all counted on Rob to have those Snicker bars. Spring or fall, 11a.m. can be downright hot in West Texas. Sweat is running freely and the morning hits a lull. We punch through and usually work the last calf close to 12:30 p.m. Then it's a small hike to begin the bathroom shifts to clean up for lunch.

* * *

The foreman's house with its chain link fenced yard, the barn, sheds, and stock pens is settled among a scatter of oaks. Folding tables and chairs are set out in the courtyard among the roses and irises-some as old as me. In Texas irises are one of the hardiest plants around. You will often see old homesteads crumbled in on themselves with plenty of irises still waving their green leaf banners to indicate what once was a home still has the spirit. Outside the chain link fence an occasional escaped chicken clucks around the dirt and grass looking for bugs. Dogs are barking but rarely allowed in during mealtime. Boots and chaps have come off, and the laughter is beginning to rise. This is the time when the cowboys take no mercy by reiterating all the mistakes of the morning. And next are the stories of their escapades on other ranches. The hemming and hawing crescendos in tales of hilarious antics, and of course, the storyteller keeps such a straight dumb face it's even harder to stop laughing.

Finally all the food is set out and Arlon, who is also a pastor, says a prayer. His words are etched on my heart and recorded on my phone. "All loving and merciful Father in heaven, we thank thee for this day and all the blessings of this life. We realize Heavenly Father that every good and perfect gift cometh down from thee. So we thank thee for this day for all blessings, for health, for strength, for proper exercise, our minds and bodies and food and clothing and shelter. Today Heavenly Father, we want to especially thank thee for this association, for this friendship, for the families, especially for the Beckham family and for their generosity down through the years and for their attitude and for being friends and helpful to everybody. We want to thank thee Heavenly Father for all thy many blessings. We thank thee for this food that we might all enjoy. We pray that thy will be with us. Give us safe trips. Guide, guard, and direct us. Thank thee for the rains and we pray if it be thy will may we receive some more. We pray in Christ's name, Amen."

Everyone I love is gathered in the courtyard for good food and shared joy. Angelica's spread includes a delicious brisket, green beans with slabs of bacon floating in liquid, rice, pinto beans, tossed salad, and her famous homemade tortillas and even more famous hot hot sauce. There is sweet tea or regular. And always a dessert, usually a slab cake with way too much frosting. We sit around the folding tables and catch up on children, college, and UT football. My nieces and nephews all live very vibrant and full lives. Being together allows us to hear each other's victories and concerns.

Dr. Rob frames it this way, "Roundups are something special. It's like the best kind of family reunion because you're working together. There's nothing like getting in the pens with my parents, siblings, cousins, aunts, and uncles and working towards the same objective. We're all breathing in the same dirt, we're all getting kicked in the legs and stepped on our toes, and we all get to enjoy a feast together after the work is done! It may be the single most powerful thing that has made me feel connected and close to my extended family."

The following quietness signals that most have begun the digestive process with a nap on the porch. As kids, we would snicker at the snoring snuffles. Then it became a game to see who could hold in their laughter. Sometimes a found feather was used to tickle a nose, which of course meant bursting out in belly laughs and running away in different directions not wanting to be caught. The lunch tradition started with Tommy's wife, Susie. We would bring meat from Abilene to be served with her renown Frito salad made with French dressing. There was cornbread and sweet tea. With Susie, we all ate inside around their kitchen table and in the living room. Naps were in recliners reserved for the cowboys and sometimes Rob. As the snoring increased, Dad and later John wrote out all the checks for a day's labor. My nephew, Alex Beckham remembers, "Roundup was always a treat just getting to spend time with my cousins, eat a great meal from Susie and get overpaid by my grandad for clipping calf ears."

* * *

In 2004 my siblings and our spouses bid on a chuckwagon cookout at the West Texas Rehab auction to honor Dad on his 70th birthday. We had the winning bid, and scheduled the cookout for spring roundup with the cowboys and some other family friends. We had them set up at the cabins halfway across the ranch and sent invitations to many not normally there. We had relatives from Albany come over. And cowboys from the past. But the most special was Dad's best friend, Jim Alexander. Jim and Dad played football together in Junior High School. They served in the Army in Georgia. And they were both ranchers doing many cattle deals as partners. Jim and Jerri, his wife, were my godparents and I always knew they were looking out for me. Their son, Mike, followed in his dad's footsteps. John and Mike spent a lot of time learning ranching, fishing and hunting; they were the next generation forging strong bonds of friendship. Our families were connected and spent many weekends doing life alongside each other. To see Jim and Dad sitting on the porch revisiting days gone by just pulled at my heart. It is bittersweet when older friends spend time together. Between them exists all the hopes and dreams along with the tragedies.

Roundups weren't the only food fellowships. My nephew, Bryson Beckham remembers spending Thanksgiving eating together with family, and watching football with Nonnie and Grandad. He remembers Susie's peach cobbler and Tommy's firm handshake. Lynn has had several Thanksgiving gatherings with her tribe and the smiles in the photos prove it was a delicious feast. In 2007, Mom wrote the following note;

Thanksgiving at the ranch with Lynn, Robert, Jeff, Justin, Rob, Julie, Bryson, Alex and Austin. Cold, cold, cold with snow after a mild fall. Six inches on the ground in Abilene but only a scattering here. Alex shot a seven point buck, great excitement. Bryson saw an eight point, but they watched it trail a doe until it was an impossible shot. Rutting season and the bucks aren't too alert to hunters. Big dinner up at the big house. Watched the Cowboys maul the NY Jets setting up a big game with Green Bay. Bob drove to the lake to winterize the house and then we will head home for the Longhorn - Aggie game. Julie and Rob are driving to Austin for a second Thanksgiving. Lots of birds but too cold to get out. Seen from the cabin: cardinals, chickadees, juncos, Harris's sparrows, rufous-sided towhees, and a crow.

The family cabins have hosted much warmth and wonder. My favorite was a meal with Jay and my parents. We wanted to do something special and we knew how much Dad liked BBQ shrimp from Pascal's

Manale's in New Orleans. The family had flown it in on past occasions. Jay, being an excellent cook, researched the recipe. He did all the prep work to get the freshest shrimp and served an excellent rendition of it. We even had handwipes to handle the mess. There was something miraculous in eating a loved meal in a loved location. And there was a shift in our relationship. We were two couples having a shared date. We were best of friends. Sometimes it feels like heaven lies just beyond the veil of this everyday world.

* * *

The cabins lay nestled among a circle of big live oaks. The first was the little cabin, a log version with wood floors containing my parents' bedroom and ours with four bunk beds. It was just enough for one family. Then as we married and expanded our numbers, the big cabin was built up the road from what was now to be called Mom and Dads' cabin. The area around the cabins had been loosely sculpted to allow for a playground and sandbox which has passed on as our kids grew. This is a sacred space for community gathering and private retreat. Mom loved to spend time at the ranch and we all cherish the special holidays like Easter spent tucked away in the hills. Impromptu worship services were conducted with Carolyn Beckham, my sister-in-law, often playing the guitar. And even though the children were anxious to start hunting eggs, they were mesmerized by the sweet strumming of her chords. Those times also included celebrating the sacrament of communion and the deep meaning of our relationship with Jesus. Those moments are now even more cherished as the generations have changed.

Looking back, I now recognize another communion meal we have called chips and salsa. A college friend once looked in my mom's refrigerator and dubbed her the queen of condiments. There were always no less than three jars of salsa, but you better check the expiration date. This was a diet staple and it was a prerequisite during time on the porch before the dinner meal. It was even more necessary if hunting or fishing had been part of the earlier day. She had a special dish with a partition for the chips and another for the salsa. In fact we all got one for Christmas. John recalls coming in after hunting to enjoy these appetizers in front of the fire – always a fire even when the outside temperature was in the 70s. Dad showed his love to Mom by humoring her with fires whenever she wanted them. This cozy and comfortable cabin with a fire blazing on the hearth, convinced us that the dark night and the howling coyotes were shut out and all was well.

Food ushered in the sacredness of our everyday moments. We could count on Mom to have a surplus of mints, gum, mini candy bars, and German gummy bears. Lynn and I often tease each other with a salute to Mom's never ending purse of sweets and Kleenex.

The sentimental nourishment extended off the ranch also. There were those lunchtime Robertson's ham sandwiches, two pieces of white bread and ham from Baird. If you wanted any condiments, you better grab them quickly from the packets because Dad never wanted to wait long. Soft ice cream from Dairy Queen was less frequent but always hoped for on a ride back to town. And Emily's favorite, after a day of horseback riding with her dad, is the Clyde Whataburger. She says a burger never tasted better.

WTRC Chuckwagon

Cake!

Bob Beckham and a grandson.

Six

Wildlings Work

Ready to brand.

DAYS OF SUMMER

That they may be called trees of righteousness,
The planting of the Lord, that He may be glorified.
Isaiah 61:3b

SUMMER AT THE RANCH is as hot as a firecracker. The scrub has lost its spring softness. Prickly undergrowth will grab your legs and slow any hike. Which makes one wonder if jeans would have been a better choice than shorts. The days of summer start and end with heat. There is no cool morning unless it has rained. Those summer seasons were spent living on the ranch, with John, in a mobile home that was meant to develop my work ethic. It was old and battered from being dragged across many pastures and finally settled about a mile away from head-quarters in what was to become the Cabin Trap. John started working there years before me staying in a little camper trailer under the trees at the windmill in the Uncle George pasture. He recalls, working all day, cooking a light meal, then showering after which he would go sit in a lawn chair and stare out at the heavens, the stars and the moon. It was a time to ponder. There were no TVs, cell phones, or other diversions – just books to read and creation to look out upon. Waking up with a snake in his bed is what I remember. Luckily it was a "good" snake and I think it prompted Dad to get the larger mobile home.

My summer work included walking cedar post fence lines and pulling up the loose barbed wire. Tying it off. Then moving to the next cedar post to do it all over again. Today our fences are built with steel T-posts and strung tightly by crews, trained and efficient. My summer hours were marked by the cedar posts and the rising temperature of the blazing sun. Lunch was packed so there was no real break in the day. My body ached and angry thoughts of the unfair situation raged. On the second or third day a miracle occurred. The rhythm of the day became a lullaby in quietness. The noise in my head stopped as if it had completely run out of gas and had nothing more to say. The drama slipped away and I experienced the perfect tranquility of post after post. The low hanging branches that tangled my hair were deftly avoided as if I was one with the land. Fallen logs that once blocked my way became resting places for a cool drink and a moment to listen. The quietness was filled with the voices of cardinals, turkey, and an occasional bobwhite quail. These days were creating a deeper sense of belonging. They were knitting my heart with the ranch and bringing me into my own heart. The wisdom of my dad to put us out there for weeks at a time shaped and formed the people we are today. And he didn't stop with our generation. He extended that opportunity to our children.

Donald says, "On the ranch Grandad was always glad to have us grandkids free range and roam as far as we wanted. I don't think I ever heard him tell me to stop before a certain point, just to be careful of snakes. Now I see how Grandad was growing our sense of adventure and independence. I also remember working for him in the summers running the 4-wheeler and herbicide to keep the cedar trees down."

* * *

The following paragraphs share memories from John's sons, Dr. Rob and Michael Beckham's summer occupation as ranch hands for foreman Tommy Rogers. They are written alternating back and forth.

"Michael and I worked for a few weeks every summer between the ages of 12 and 18 at the ranch under Tommy's supervision. Some of my most cherished memories are from those summers." —Dr. Rob

When I think of the ranch, I feel peace and contentment. I remember curiosity and exploration, the anxiety of getting lost, and the confidence gained of finding my way back. I think of coming of age with my brother. I think of the men I admire, who shaped me. —writes Michael

"These times were also where I came to appreciate Tommy's patience and gentleness. I have failed Tommy countless times—sleeping in through my alarm, dropping the sucker rod down the shaft, getting lost and taking three times longer to get back after putting out cattle feed, shoddy welding jobs, shallow post holes, and the list goes on and on. Despite this, I can only think of one time where Tommy visibly showed his disappointment. It was the time Michael and I lost his family heirloom pliers. Tommy sent us to the Red Tank to patch the western fence line. We did not have our own tools, so he gave us two sets of pliers. After finishing walking the entire fence line, we were getting close to running out of water. Being the young geniuses that we were, we decided instead of walking the fence back, which would have taken us west, south, and then east again to get back to the truck, we would just take a shortcut directly south through the brush of the Red Tank. Of course, this did not turn out well. We quickly got lost and spent hours pushing through thick brush until we eventually happened upon the electric well, which was a sight for sore eyes since we had been out of water for several hours at that point. Eventually, we made it back to Tommy's house, and we realized we were missing one set of pliers. We thought it would be simple enough to order some new ones and give them to him, but when we told Tommy which set was missing, he suddenly looked painfully disappointed. He did not get angry with us but explained that he had found those pliers on a washed-out road and they were meaningful to him; one day, he planned to give them to Kendra, his daughter. Tommy was very patient and did not let us dwell on the subject, but Michael and I could tell he was disappointed. The next summer, when we had some free time, Michael and I decided to try and retrace our steps to find the pliers. Miraculously, we seemed to have retraced the exact chaotic steps through all that hilly brush and actually found the pliers. I'll never forget the look of joy on Tommy's face when we pulled them out and put them in his hands." —Dr. Rob

When I think of the ranch, I am back in a small trailer lying on the creaky springs of a twin mattress, waking up next to my brother. Dad's not out here with us anymore, it's just us, and we'd better hurry so we're not late for breakfast at Tommy's. I think of losing Tommy's pliers, given to him long ago and meaningful to him, and retracing our steps across an open field for hours until we found them. —writes Michael

"There was a moment that Michael and I had to patch a really long fence line in the Red Tank pasture. It took way longer than either of us anticipated. I remember feeling so exhausted afterwards and was longing for the comforts of home. When we finally got back to Old Blue, we popped open the cooler which had two half-frozen Gatorades. We sat in the truck bed and sipped on those cold Gatorades as it started to rain on us. Michael and I looked at each other and smiled. It was a holy moment. I could feel God making his face shine upon us." —Dr. Rob

When I think of the ranch, I'm sitting on a ridge in the Red Tank in the back of Old Blue, drinking a Gatorade with my brother after a hard day repairing fence in the high heat of summer, suddenly overcome with giddy joy by a surprise rainstorm, so cool on our faces, the whole world smelled fresh again. —writes Michael

* * *

Summer's intense heat allows the hammering of character on the anvil of despair. There are valuable lessons that only failure can teach. Getting lost in a pasture, running out of water, and always being snake aware are not easy, comfortable ways to spend a summer vacation. The schooling the ranch offers is small trials and triumphs. A tight five-strand barbed-wire fence after a day's work imparts confidence. It builds identity.

* * *

Cattle round ups are the main avenue of learning how to work at the ranch. They involve community and generational teaching. We are passing on the mantle of stewarding the land and ranch. In 2008, Mom wrote a note describing all the ways the grandchildren were working.

> Spring roundup has been a great family time with most of the family working. Donald here with Sally before leaving for Okinawa for three years. Sad for us but exciting for him. Sarah here from Tech shocking the calves. Emily was castrating and covered with blood. Donald pushing calves through the chute. Bryson and Austin helping in the pens. It was a very special Mother's Day on Sunday. John joined me at the eight o'clock service at church. Donald showed a slideshow of his Marine training. Kids are all learning to play gin rummy. I beat Emily at backgammon (rare), but she trounced me at gin—and I was teaching her! Lots of martins. Two Mississippi kites, nest must be nearby, cowbirds—sad face, phoebe nest on porch, cardinals, turkey and deer. Bob killed a huge rattlesnake at the northeast corner of the yard, 11 rattles!

As an adult I view the work differently than as a child. Seeing the bigger picture, gives an opening to pray into the atmosphere, to seek God's will. There is a connection felt among those who have gone before us and those of us still here. For a child, everything they are doing is teaching them how to be an adult, successful or not. Emily shared this and I was reminded of how play is a life lesson and everything they were doing was guiding them as they grew up. "A cherished memory is all the times my mom, Carolyn Beckham, would make us a picnic lunch. My brothers, Michael and Rob, and I would all set out and walk to Deer Pond to build forts out of the cedar branches along the washes near the pond and hunt for arrowheads. Nothing tasted quite as good as eating our pb&j sandwiches inside our newly made forts!"

Michael, describes it this way; "I think of whole days of my childhood spent digging into a dirt cliff in the Richardson near Deer Pond with my siblings and cousins. We were chopping off cedar branches to cover the roof and door, a village of dugouts to fend off attacks. We could survive anything together."

Alex remembers going to the ranch with his little league baseball team. "We spent our days building forts out of whatever we could find and running all over the property playing capture the flag. It was loud, sweaty, and carefree in the way only 12 year-old boys can be."

One generation to the next.

Teamwork!

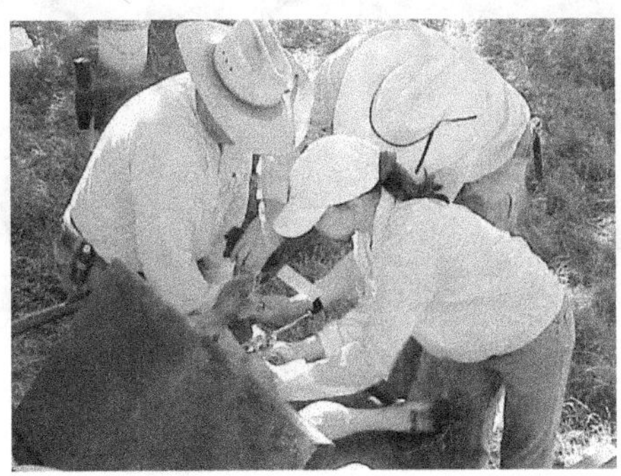

Birds, Bees, and Butterflies

Nonnie

NONNIE'S LEGACY

For lo, the winter is past, the rain is over and gone.
The flowers appear on the earth; the time of singing has come,
Song of Solomon 2:11

"Petit à petit, l'oiseau fait son nid."

THE FRENCH PROVERB was one of the many framed pieces of art on Peggy Beckham's prayer wall, which means: "Little by little, the bird builds its nest." It's a metaphor for patience and persistence, showing that complex tasks are often accomplished through many small, consistent actions, writes my daughter, Sarah Capra Seltzer. She continues; on the wall surrounding the French proverb, and throughout my grandparents' house, many paintings, photos, and sculptures of hummingbirds were displayed. And, more often than not, a quick glance in the backyard would result in a hummingbird sighting - amongst the beautiful flower beds, or any of the many hummingbird feeders that were always freshly filled with sweet, sticky sugar-water for their enjoyment.

In my growing-up years, I had the unique privilege of accompanying Grandad, on his weekly drive out to the ranch. There he would let his bird dogs run, check on cattle, visit the foreman, and usually include a quick stop at the cabin, where he would water the grass directly in front of the cabin, fill the bird baths, suet cake cages, and bird feeders. We would usually eat a sandwich while sitting on the porch swing, giving the dogs time to hydrate, and giving Grandad time to make a batch of hummingbird food and refill the bird feeders. I remember being curious why he took the time to do this – no one lived in this particular cabin full-time, so why make such an effort to water the grass, or attract birds to that location? It wasn't until I was spending one of many weekends with Nonnie and Grandad at the ranch cabin that I began to understand Grandad's weekly cabin-chores routine.

Perhaps it was an especially harsh winter that year, or perhaps it had recently rained after a long dry-period; but I know this had to be a weekend in mid- to late-spring after a shift in the weather pattern based on the drastic change in scenery and surroundings since Grandad and I had been there the week before. What had been dry, muted shades of brown and gray landscape, were now fresh, crisp greens, speckled heavily with bright yellow, red, and blue flowers. The small yard in front of the cabin was bright green underneath and blue across the top – the shorter grass being overshadowed by the thick layer of taller bluebonnets which blanketed the fenced-in space. All along the porch and in the trees surrounding the cabin, the bird feeders provided a gathering hub for a vast diversity of winged creatures. We spent most of that weekend on the porch or walking around the cabin, with Nonnie identifying the different types of birds, either by their looks or their calls, and then practicing to see if we could mimic them or get them to speak back to us.

Most memorable to me, now thirty-something years later, were the hummingbirds coming in for their sugar-water treat, and wondering how such a tiny creature could move so quickly and with such grace all around us. A self-described "near-sighted lover of nature," Nonnie constantly shared her deep appreciation of the natural world around us during our time spent together at the ranch. Grandad, like-minded in this appreciation, consistently ensured the small background tasks were accomplished, so that together they, (and their grandchildren), could enjoy the magnificent beauty in a field of bluebonnets, a bird's song, or a hummingbird hovering in time.

Donald's experience was a little different. "Nonnie was a bird watcher. I was a young boy who couldn't sit still for more than 30 seconds. These are not very compatible states. However, I do remember on a couple of occasions sitting with her on the front porch swing at the cabin and watching a flock of turkeys come to the feeder. I also remember a time when it was rainy, and sitting on the same swing Nonnie and I listened to the different songbirds and tried to identify them."

The funniest story comes from Dr. Rob. One spring they were out at the ranch for Easter. Emily, Michael, and he had some Cadbury chocolate eggs and found an empty nest. They picked out the candy eggs that looked just like Robin's eggs and put a few of them in the nest. Then they called Nonnie outside exclaiming how they had found a nest and she needed to see it. When she came out, she became excited, teaching them how they were Robin's eggs. Suddenly Emily, Michael, and Dr. Rob each reached in and grabbed an egg and popped it in their mouth! He describes a look of horror on Nonnie's face followed by relief and so much laughter as she realized the joke they had played on her.

* * *

"Weekend escapes to the ranch are something sacred." describes Julie Beckham, my sister -in-law, "With Rob and our friends, I learned what it meant to slow down. We hunted arrowheads and fossils baked into the red dirt by time, rode horses across open pastures, watched wildflowers stretch endlessly across the land each spring, and counted the stars that were crisp and clear at night. Yes, the sky at the Spring Gap Ranch is that wide! Birds filled the mornings with sounds I did not know how to name. In the Fall, the leaves turned every shade of gold, rust, and fire. I learned to shoot clays, to sit quietly and observe the birds and wildlife. I learned how a cattle ranch works: how cattle are moved, how the land is respected, and how stewardship is a way of life, not just a word."

* * *

We spend much of our lives tending, keeping, and caring. Nonnie taught us to live a birdsong life. To appreciate every moment especially those where birds of every sort twitter and dart through the branches of the cottonwood and nearby trees. The Spring Gap Ranch is a composer of seasonal songs. It is magnificent from winter to spring and from late summer into fall. The wildflowers and budding trees, with just a few well timed rains, jumpstart the flora to life. A beautiful reminder of how God provides all we need. March's bright pink hello of the redbud trees turns to April's magnificent blanket of bluebonnets. In May, Carolyn loves to pick handfuls of pastel colored Indian blankets and black-eyed Susan to adorn a table. And very soon after that, Dad's favorite would burst forth in bright crimson glory. As I drove him to the ranch in his later years, we would calculate who would spot the first standing cypress flowers. He had the advantage of knowing from past years where the clumps were located. And he had probably, secretly been watching for their tall green stalks. Flowers attract pollinators. The mesquite blooms along with the spring flowers offer a heavy aroma. Thus making the ranch a sanctuary for bees and butterflies. A seed is a beginning and an end. It is the first stage of a new plant and the final offering of a dried up bloom. In the Beckham and Capra families we have a long history with honey bees. Jay wrote the following account.

One of my first memories of Bob, when Nancy and I were still dating, has to do with bees and harvesting honey. I wasn't aware that raising bees was a thing on the ranch. Nancy and I came to Abilene one week-end and when we pulled into her parent's driveway the bees were flying everywhere. Bob was bent over a white wooden frame with his hot knife filling the air with a sweet honey smoke. Nancy was quite excited and said something like, Dad's harvesting honey! So we pitched in and I helped spin the centrifuge inside a giant metal can with a spigot on the bottom. Once the crank got hard to spin, Bob said we had enough honey to start filing jars. This went on for at least an hour. Gallons of honey were harvested that day and I was hooked. I later saw the hives on a hillside outside the foreman's house. Sometime in the future Bob hung up his honey business and put all the equipment in storage.

Years later when our kids were in 4-H we resurrected beekeeping as a family project. I cleaned up the old hives and Nancy was able to procure a queen and some bees from a local beekeeper. Over the next decade that grew into three working hives and all the kids helped harvest the honey. We were able to clean and use the same centrifuge extractor that was Bobs! Local honey is a prized gift and we gave a lot away over those years. Eventually all but one of the hives died out and I forgot about it until we moved out of that house and into town. I carefully moved that hive out to the Richardson pasture. Nancy and I were able to harvest it twice over the next three years and then it died off.

The hive sat empty and I didn't think about it again until four years ago when Rob noticed bee activity in the same hive! I opened it up, cleaned the old frames and added some fresh frames. We have since harvested it three more times. That volunteer hive is still going strong today!

Our moments and our months are distinguished by the color of the trees. The seasons shifting, the clouds coming and going, the trees budding, blooming, greening, coloring, falling. Advent, Epiphany, Lent, Pentecost. The Spring Gap is splattered with red oaks, sumac, and cottonwoods that dominate the fall canvas. Like a patchwork quilt of color the ranch lays itself out in beauty. Nature is singing a song, the trees are clapping their hands, and we are called to join them. The towering cottonwood tree on the stream bank welcomes the turkeys to roost. Wide mesquite prairies are studded with clumps of prickly pear that grow wide and tall. We fall in love with the enchanting beauty and mysterious scents.

Carolyn speaks of the monarch tree where a million orange wings rest overnight. It is a phenomenon that occurs in October as they migrate south for the winter. The Spring Gap is often on the migratory route of monarch butterflies. The migration is a relay, with successive generations moving northward in the spring, breeding along the way, while the final fall generation makes the long trip to Mexico. This "super generation" journeys south to overwinter, while returning north in spring. Unlike summer generations that live three to five weeks, this generation lives up to eight months to complete the migration and overwintering cycle. One year they chose to stay overnight in a large oak outside our little cabin. My nephew, Jeff Davis, was there. He was close to 12 years old and was spending the weekend with Nonnie and Grandad. He surely received a tutorial from Nonnie on the scientific event that was happening, but the most amazing thing was the wonder he experienced in that thrilling moment when thousands of butterflies dipped and fluttered around him. He physically raised his arms in praise and the photograph, while now faded, still expresses his pure joy. His mother, Lynn talks about many years of going out with Mom and Dad and learning about nature. That's where she found and was blessed to have such a love for nature— and she saw God in all of it. Surrounded by His creation is definitely where she feels closest to our Maker. Jeff died in 2013. He is missed at roundups and every holiday that passes. His birthday was in October making the butterfly migrations even more significant.

Birds, butterflies, and bees are connected. To one another, and to us. Sometimes we trample their messages like scattered leaves beneath our feet. Learning to pause gets easier with age. I want to observe the ordinary things of earth and receive their messages, to hear and see with inner knowing. Like an everyday liturgy declaring aliveness, wholeness, spirit, and grace —the Spring Gap Ranch is a place where beauty and peace take root, flourish, and thrive. A growing work of creation, endless in its changing elements. The story of creation has love as its theme. This is the peace of shalom, a Hebrew word meaning wholeness and harmony. It is a beauty we tend but did not create. We steward and seek His will in these everyday moments.

Monarch Butterflies

Eight

Dawn and Dusk

Maxbo Tex

SILENCE THEN SOUND

While the earth remains:
Seedtime and harvest, cold and heat,
Winter and summer, and day and night shall not cease.
Genesis 8:22

"BE QUIET, BE STILL, LISTEN!"
These words were spoken over me many times as I sat with my dad learning to observe wildlife. As a child, I was expected to be outside. To explore and make connections. Now as an adult, I retreat to the ranch to rest and to be restored. There is no greater stewardship that occurs at the Spring Gap than that of the wildlife and habitat. Aldo Leopold, a visionary conservationist, wrote in A Sand County Almanac;

> Wildlife is never destroyed except as the soil itself is destroyed; it is simply converted from one form to another. You cannot prevent soil from growing plants, nor can you prevent plants from feeding animals. The only question is: What kind of plants? What kind of animals? How many? (Leopold 70)

These are questions that we ask. Dad always said a rancher is a farmer of grass. Out in the hills are white-tail deer, rabbits, skunks, racoons, bobcats, coyotes, hogs, and maybe even a mountain lion. Along the creeks where the cottonwoods grow are flocks of wild turkey. For each of these species it's important to know animal anatomy and behavior together with population dynamics, nutrition, botany and habitat management which all play a part in keeping the balance. The most destructive animals on the ranch are the wild hogs. They are highly prolific, with females reaching sexual maturity as early as six to eight months and producing one to two litters annually of four to twelve piglets each. With a gestation period of roughly 115 days, they can breed year-round, allowing populations to double in as little as four months. They root and forage the land unmercifully. They destroy small trees, planted crops, and fences. They compete with other wildlife and livestock and very quickly can overrun the carrying capacity of the ranch.

Leopold is also considered the father of game management and he established the five tools for habitat management: the axe, cow, plow, fire, and gun. Each of these tools can be used to add or detract from the habitat. Donald spent an extensive time on the ranch evaluating the health of our land and populations. He participated in the Texas Quail Index, a statewide program in 2002. The goal was to predict the causes of quail decline and produce management strategies to reverse it. He writes the following.

Nothing can compare with the beauty of a covey of bobwhite quail flushing on a morning when the air has chilled enough to see both your own and the bird's breath. I feel a thrill when I hear the beating wings as they rise to make an escape. I often trailed dogs with Grandad who had a passion for hunting. He believed that the future of the ranch rested upon our livestock and wildlife management working together. He stewarded the ranch to benefit both. I had never thought about the many different ways that we can help the public understand the important role that hunters play in wildlife conservation. If everyone who loves wildlife invested in natural resource management the way hunters do, we could paint a brighter future for them in Texas.

The Spring Gap Ranch has been a blessing that allowed me to learn and grow in the areas of responsibility, gratitude, respect, and value. Responsibility for the livestock, the wildlife, the people, and the land which all interact at different levels. Gratitude for the freedom of space and means to play and grow, to explore and create. Respect for the past decisions and wisdom of others who maintained the ranch as a whole. Finally the value of land and the anchoring influence it can have on family as well as the ability to bless others. I'm not sure I have felt more peaceful and awed at creation than when hunting on the ranch. Sitting under a tree on a hill, as the sun rises, and the early radiation fog burns away to reveal the creek bed and valley below. Seeing the animals wandering and making their way between the foliage. A deep sense of calm and eternal perspective comes from considering the slowly changing nature of the land and the creatures that inhabit it, and the briefness of our earthly lives similar to the morning's misty vapors. Hunting allows me to continue to walk the land and see the wildlife. I think I can gauge the ranch health by the number and kinds of animals I see, the growth states of the plants, and how wet or dry it "feels". Now that I have children who are starting to hunt, I am able to begin passing on the valuable lessons and joys that I originally experienced decades ago.

* * *

The hunting season starts in the fall for deer and the spring for turkey. The best time to observe wildlife is at dawn and before dusk. We don't overhunt the ranch and have guidelines on what should be taken. When the hunters first crawl out of bed the whippoorwills, owls, and other night birds are still calling. In the fall, the yellow leaves dance across the branches. It feels as if something beautiful at the heart of creation is revealed. It feels like an embrace. The world is saturated with meaning. Autumn's glorious canopy roars its final hope before winter's still whispers settle in. Rarely do we know what is at stake when beauty surprises us into stillness and we pause to listen, even for a moment, to creation's song. This is the way of the morning. We walk with God expecting signs and wonders. There was a weekend that Jay and I spent at the ranch with the specific idea to hike into the box canyon in the Richardson pasture. It was slow going as we were basically following the water trail uphill. It was exciting to pick our way through greenbriar avoiding poison ivy and balance moving upward. Like pioneers scoping out a future hideaway from Indian attacks we continued on. The climb up into the cavern of the canyon was quite steep and the rocks were more like boulders. As we were ascending, I heard a menacing sound, like a growl and bark. Jay was ahead of me and a bit higher. Suddenly I remembered the story he had told me about a hunting trip with Dad and how a mountain lion crossed their path fairly close to where we were. "Don't go any farther, we're invading something's territory." I whispered. Well that only increased Jay's curiosity. Another strange sound and I was out of there praying he would make it safely back to the RTV. Of course nothing happened and whatever was making those sounds decided to lay low. A mountain lion has a large home range from 25 to 100 square miles. There have been sightings and even some shot in communities close to the ranch, though it is rare.

> Gosh--it turned me into a hunter!!
> And a fairly good one at that!

Says Sally Capra, my daughter-in-law, when asked how the ranch changed her. "Even in years that are busy, or chaotic, Donald and I have a standing date every November to go deer hunting together. I love spending time with my husband, on the ranch, in the still and quiet mornings. And Donald is so kind as to be patient with me: he always lets me shoot first, and he always field-dresses my deer for me. Nonnie was probably one of the most influential people into why I hunt. She was such an encourager of stewarding the land and the wildlife, but always just thought it was "so cool" that I would go out with Donald to hunt deer. She would ask every year about our hunts, and championed when I harvested one for our family's freezer. I loved having her cheering me on!"

* * *

My nephew, Bryson Beckham, said, "My favorite memories of the ranch are the many hours spent hunting with my dad and brothers. As a kid I remember getting restless and bored in the quiet morning hours, but as an adult I feel blessed to have had so much peaceful time with family." His dad, Rob, has been a forerunner in many areas but especially on the ranch. He championed uses for aerial craft that got everyone's hearts beating faster. He flew an experimental craft with my mom and then my dad. Mom loved her flight, Dad not so much. I guess the difference in weights was the reason he nearly clipped an electric line. Rob designed and built waterways on the east side of the ranch that flow throughout the year. And water is a big deal on the ranch. But his most inspired enterprise was his deer business. I asked him to write the synopsis which follows.

> One of the newer agricultural endeavors at the Spring Gap has been to add to the whitetail population. Back in 2001 and 2002 Dad commissioned a deer census. This was done with a Vietnam War era helicopter. In 2001, we counted 201 deer and in 2002, we counted 207. This was a very disappointing population and explained why we did not see many deer. The few bucks we did see were not very majestic in size or crown. This puzzled me because our ranch seemed to be the ideal environment for the whitetail to flourish.
>
> As a family we have bred cattle, dogs, goats, etc. Why not deer? In 2006, I researched how to go about getting a permit and visited with a friend that was stocking his ranch with some South Texas deer. This idea soon grew into a passion and a business for 20 years.

In the beginning, we selected some buck semen from some big breeder bucks from Oklahoma and Ohio. I bought 6 does from good stock and my friends, Gil Deshazo and Cactus Schroeder each bought 6 does, so we were set to artificially inseminate our eighteen does. I had some pens built and I found a guy with a mobile lab that he backed up to the gate.

The idea was that we would run them down the alley and into a compartment. Well, that wasn't how it went at all. We first had to get them out of the pen. It was well past sunset and our pen was full of basketball size rocks. We all had flashlights but that just informed the deer where we were. They went round and round, avoiding the gate at all costs. We were lined up and trying to push them to the gate. Gil was next to the fence on the west side when a doe ran him over. All I saw was his flashlight flipping in the air, followed by a loud thud and grunt.

We finally got them in the alley, by this time the moon was high overhead and had an ominous red tint to it. My brother, John, grabbed me by jacket and said, "What have you got me into brother!"

We did finally get them all worked and over the years we have made many modifications in how we move the deer through the process. It is much more humane for the animals and especially the people. Early on, I released many of the offspring of the deer onto the ranch but in 2011, the state of Texas made it illegal to release breeder pen deer on a low fence ranch. By then, we had raised some truly spectacular deer and there was a strong market for them. Instead of releasing them, we sold them to nearby high fence ranches.

In the last few years, the regulatory climate has gotten so bad that the economics are no longer positive. We high fenced a little over 700 acres on the east side and I have been releasing our deer so that the genetics will live on at the Spring Gap Ranch. It has been a wild ride with many fond memories!

* * *

Dad was kind enough to stock the ranch tanks with several different varieties of fish. And nature itself added to that population. Both my parents loved to fish and it is one of the things I love about my husband, Jay. He says fishing with the grandkids has reminded him of our own kids catching fish in the same tanks 30 years ago. It is quite a thrill when your seven year old granddaughter catches a catfish she can't lift out of the water. Austin remembers fishing with Grandad at the Blue Tank as something he will always carry with him. Just sitting there, catching fish, and enjoying the scenery.

Jennifer Davis, Jeff's widow and my niece, put it this way, "I cherish the moments spent exploring the ranch, learning about nature and the history of the land, lending a hand at roundup, hanging out with family, and watching our children do all of the same. I love seeing our children enjoy the ranch just as Jeff always did. Spring Gap has taught me to slow down, enjoy the quiet of nature, and to savor every moment spent with the ones you love. I will forever treasure the precious memories made at the ranch, and look forward to creating many more for years to come."

* * *

There have been many challenges as the energy sector has changed. Wind turbine companies have approached us many times and our answer has been no. They do not manage them well, and they are an eyesore to the natural landscape. They also make continuous noise which irritates the cattle and livestock, along with people. Our experience with workers coming on and off our land is they do not respect it. Gates are left open which is dangerous for our livestock. The newest threat is a high capacity electric line. We are praying that it not go across our ranch for many of those same reasons.

Carolyn says, "Thankfully, the ranch land itself has not changed much over the years. The expansive canyons and vistas, except for some distant tall windmills, have remained virtually the same. And that was by intention, to keep the land raw and untamed for future generations to enjoy. The addition of many new tanks is especially welcome. How fun to watch them rise and fall as we celebrate a good downpour on the land!"

While a good rain is always welcome, the reality of dry years has brought stress. Mom wrote in a poem, "The shank of summer is upon us. Scorpio settles in her western bed. Dust devils hopscotch over the sun-baked, mud-caked turtle shell of earth." This hard reality of parched land holds true in West Texas. When we were kids, Dad would notice a summer thunderhead cloud in the sky. He would round us all up and order us out to the front yard. And this was in a neighborhood where everyone knew everyone and people were outside. We then proceeded to make a dance circle and started hootin and hollerin pretending to be Indians performing a rain dance. Sometimes our neighborhood friends would join in but mostly they just stared. Dad must have released some worry because the years of drought passed and on those rare occasions that rain came after a dance, we all felt a little accomplished.

The ranch is full of beauty and decay, untimely ends and new beginnings, promises and possibilities. Weather fronts move through and begin to cool the air. Evenings are drawing in and trees are going bare. We lean into the rhythm of each season. The hazy saddleback of Buzzard Peak, once a camping place of Comanche Indians, hides a narrow pass of greenbriar that leads to innumerable natural joys and wonder. The splendor of an early evening hike draws me closer to God with the sideoats brushing my boots and the setting sun on my back. It is easy to reflect on the glory and the majesty of the Creator. Here we live according to the ebb and flow. Places change us as we go about changing them. As I walk along the brow of a hill on this clear night when the air is still and cold, I am grateful to care for this God-created ground beneath my feet.

Grandaddy Bass and a Natural Trophy

Nine

Fire

AND ICE

He who forms mountains, and creates the wind,
Who declares to man what His thought is,
and makes the morning darkness,
Who treads the high places of the earth
—The Lord God of hosts is His name.
Amos 4:13

IT WAS LATE AFTERNOON when the phone rang. The voice on the other end said, "The ranch is on fire!" Those words were both paralyzing and rocketing. There is no choice other than to immediately pull on boots and jacket and head out the door. We all met within ten minutes and loaded into the truck with Dad. It was an unwanted reunion but also comforting to be with all my siblings. This drive was even more frenzied than mornings of roundups because this drive was life or death and animals were our highest priority. As we turned off I-20 and headed towards the gap we could see smoke rising in the far distance. That also created great concern because it meant the fire was big.

There were no conversations because we were all praying. Once we got on the ranch we headed towards the smoke, now an angry billow blowing across the pasture. Volunteer fire departments were arriving and cattle were being secured away from the flames and the direction the fire was moving. As the situation was being assessed we made plans to evacuate the most precious things in the family cabins as they were directly in the path of the fire. Because it was so late in the day the fire was being fought with tanker trucks and bulldozers. It moved towards the cabins and friends from other ranches started showing up with their water haulers. They sprayed the cabins as wet as they could and we continued praying.

The next morning the fire was still burning but had shifted and missed the cabins by about 20 yards. With the new day came the helicopters lifting bags of water from our tanks. That combined with the 16 volunteer fire departments along with other privately owned tanker trucks and some big 18-wheelers bringing about six large bull-dozers made them able to contain the fire. The Calvary had arrived! The acrid smell of burnt land and the searing cough from inhaling smoke are unpleasant memories from 2008. We didn't lose any cattle but the fences where the fire passed through were a loss. It burned close to 1500 acres on us in the Uncle George and Richardson pastures. Many places looked desecrated by the fire. They were a bleak landscape, scarred. The fire was started by high winds that arced electric lines, just west of us. This fire gave me an opportunity to embrace the fullness of my emotional human self and the frailty also. To be reminded of how quickly moments take a turn. And to see first-hand that heaven and earth meet in scratches and scars. It was an opportunity to experience shared life working together as a family. In West Texas it's a fight against cedars or mesquite trees. And cedars will smolder for days after the flames are gone so that any uptick in the wind brings about renewed possibilities of the fire reigniting. God created the ranch, but we continue that work and some days are more difficult than others. The outcome the following spring was quite beautiful and lush as the resurrected land burst forth in glory.

Fires can start in many ways. Lightening and discarded cigarettes are very common. Sometimes the tailpipes on older trucks can get so hot they start it up. Dr. Rob recalls one time he was driving out to the ranch just to drop something off. He had no intention of staying, so he was wearing shorts and a T-shirt with only Chaco sandals on his feet. After he dropped off the items, Tommy and he saw some smoke coming from the Red Tank. It was a small fire caused by a transformer that had blown. He grabbed a shovel and headed that way. Tommy jumped in the bulldozer. He said "I felt like a ridiculous hero in a movie in my Chacos, jumping back and forth shoveling dirt on flames while running out of the way of the bulldozer." Thankfully, the fire was small enough that they were able to contain it after about an hour. Fires like these are considered wildfires, but there is another fire that The Spring Gap was instrumental in developing. And those are called controlled burns. John writes the following remembrance from our childhood in the 1970s.

Dad, as a good steward, was always improving the ranch. He undertook a 20 year burning program with Texas Tech University to clear the cedar and improve the ranch (cattle) carrying capacity. The controlled burns conducted by Texas Tech and Dr. Henry Wright were something to witness! It would be more appropriate to say semi-controlled fires. It was a 20 year partnership with Texas Tech to essentially burn the whole ranch. The first step was bulldozing all the cedar and juniper trees and pushing the dead trees into piles. We did this pasture by pasture. Dad hired a bulldozer operator named Blanton Childress, bought a D4 Caterpillar bulldozer, and went to work. Once a pasture was pushed, we would rest it for a year to let the grass grow up so that it could carry the fire across the pasture. Then we would build fire lanes on the downwind side of the pasture that were 200 yards wide and burn out everything that was within the fire line. Then we would wait until we had a day that had perfect humidity, light winds out of the necessary direction, and a forecast of no major change in weather for the next few days. We had a lot of false starts when Dr. Wright and his team of 15 to 20 graduate students would come down and the weather would not work out. Once perfect conditions hit, the students would take off across the upwind side of the pasture with drip torches filled with kerosene and gasoline, and start the fire. This was truly an anathema to a rancher! A pasture of two thousand acres of dry, dead piles of juniper burning would create flames 40 to 50 feet and send glowing embers and smoke hundreds of feet in the air. We were lucky and had only a few minor breakouts on our neighbors' lands. The results were a ten-fold increase in the carrying capacity of cattle on the ranch and water springs coming back to life. It also opened up so much of the beauty we now enjoy.

Dr. Wright and Dad became good friends. Dr. Wright had kidney failure his last ten years of life and had to be on dialysis. When things progressed so that the dialysis was not effective anymore, he asked Dad to come up to see him in Lubbock at the hospital. On the day that Dr. Wright requested that his life-support be unplugged, he and dad had one last visit.

We don't use prescribed burning anymore. Dad told Donald certain areas become uncertain areas, and become big areas and big problems quickly. The clearing of brush in the past 15 years has been done with mechanical means making a huge improvement in the use and look of the Spring Gap Ranch. Alfredo does much of this hard work. He runs the maintainer and has dramatically improved our roads condition from mostly dirt to mostly packed caliche. He runs the bulldozer and skid steer to take out cedar and sculpt the land. One of his unique qualities is his ability to fix machinery. It is a talent and skill that has blessed the ranch.

* * *

On the other side of the nature spectrum is an event that happened in October after a roundup. This was a year that we had some yearlings, year old steers and heifers. They had been worked and were being kept at headquarters so they could be shipped out. Yearlings are known as the "teenagers". They are unpredictable and skittish. That night, also unpredicted, was an ice thunderstorm. Between the sleeting ice and the cracking thunder, these yearlings took off like crazy chaotic renegades. They completely tore down the fence and took off for Abilene. The next morning Alfredo called John, Jay, and me. We headed out to help him try and gather them up. It was slow going because the ice was thick and the roads slick. When we got to headquarters, after passing several of our herd, we got into RTV's and began the work. The cattle had run about two miles down the county road and then luckily into some land Rob owned. We got past them and then started moving them back to-wards headquarters. They were not happy. It was still freezing cold and sleeting. Jay and I were in a closed RTV with heat. Alfredo was riding a 4-wheeler. By the time we got them sequestered in a new pen he had little icicles all over. There was no complaining, just the task at hand. It was a bonding experience for us all.

As I've grown older, I realize how human nature and nature's destiny are inextricably intertwined. We respond to the crisis at hand knowing that it will be resolved. The land wages a quiet war but we belong to nature and are responsible for it. God said in Genesis to take dominion over it. It is our mandate. An amazing phenomenon on the Spring Gap Ranch are the fossils covering the landscape. The snail shells and sea urchins they once were are solidified in the limestone rocks. We are constantly seeing the miraculous right at our feet. Finding a nautilus is especially treasured. We experience seasons of making and unmaking and making anew. We live in a good world shackled by decay. A world that always seems to fall a little bit short until you spot that perfect fossil. And that is as it should be, so that we yearn for the world to come.

Ten

Sacred Spaces

said yes. Then Rob walked me over to a tree behind us where he had carved a big heart with our initials 'JRB'. And that memento is still there today. What followed has been a lifetime of meaning I could not have imagined. We have been fortunate to intentionally raise our three boys: Bryson, Alex, and Austin, near the ranch, building family memories year after year. For me and our family, the Spring Gap Ranch became more than a place, it became our 'home on the range', which has continued to give more deeply with every passing season over the years. And every time I hear that old song, "Home, Home on the Range", I smile knowing just how true it has become.

Matthew 6:10 says, "Your Kingdom come, Your will be done, on earth as it is in heaven." Julie and Rob experienced the answer to this prayer and have maintained a life dedicated to looking up.

* * *

John and Carolyn also found the ranch to be a place that nurtured and empowered their relationship. The following story comes from Carolyn.

The night was pitch black, no moon, with thousands of stars twinkling above. The smell of moisture had settled into the field in front of the little cabin. The complete absence of man-made noise was loud. This is my first memory of Spring Gap Ranch, the experience of hearing absolutely nothing. John and I wandered outside to look at the stars, away from the glow of the little cabin. He picked a yellow Primrose and put it in my hair, a flower still carefully pressed in my Bible. We walked into the middle of the field by the turkey feeder and shared the wonder of God's incredible imagination to call each star by name. Then with a perfectly straight face, he told me a "little tall tale". We had to be "very quiet" so as not to disturb the aggressive bull that was loose in the pasture. And in fact, it seemed as if I could hear some sort of animal rustling nearby, making menacing sounds. It sounded scary, so of course, I drew near so John could wrap his jacket around me.

The ranch for me is a place filled with peace, the silence of a thousand stars, a place where the seasons are on full display, and beauty praises God's name in the most creative way. And now, our children and their children and, maybe beyond, will also be mesmerized to walk out into a dark night under the stars where the only sound is a pond full of frogs, the gobble of a turkey and the howl of a coyote. And if they listen very closely, they might just hear the heavy breathing of a not-so-safe bull in the pasture beyond.

These romances speak to the great romance. How God is wooing us to draw near. To come under his jacket and rest in that security. Lynn has lived most of her life as a single mom and watching her rely on Jesus has strengthened my faith. She says we are blessed for God to have put the Spring Gap in our lives. There are no words to express the gratitude and the gifts we have learned from the land.

* * *

Jennifer says, "When we were younger, Jeff and I would drive through pastures in the dark, and sometimes even park and lay in the bed of his truck and gaze at the stars while he shared stories of the ranch from his childhood. Now, it is where I feel closest to him, as well as Nonnie and Granddad. Their spiritual presence lingers all around."

Jay and I have done several marriage vision retreats at the cabins and the presence of the Holy Spirit is thick as we dedicate that time to God and to strengthen our marriage. For Jay, the cross on the hill behind the cabins is especially sacred. It was there that we spread Mom and Dad's ashes, as a family. When the original cross deteriorated and came down Jay made it a personal project to recreate it both bigger and stronger. The new cross is made from aged redwood. Raising it was a family effort with Rob bringing his skid steer to drill a hole, and Jay bringing a tractor up the hill with concrete and water and shovels. He then made a special base decorated with ranch fossils. It was a sweet touch. We all miss my parents' presence but still feel their love. This tender memory is from John.

One spring evening, there was a spectacular sunset with white, billowing thunderclouds, some lightning and thunder in the distance, and every possible shade of pink, orange and purple imaginable. Carolyn and I persuaded mom to leave the front porch of the little cabin and drive up on Signal Hill. I opened the sunroof with mom in the passenger seat, and me in the driver's seat. I stood up in the car through the sunroof with a song about heaven playing loudly. It was a holy moment that mom would call a "thin place" where heaven almost touches Earth.

There was also a time when John was feeling fairly distant from God, he looked up at the dark sky and asked God to confirm that He was with him. He was not testing him, but wanted to see a shooting star. He waited for ten minutes, and seeing nothing, turned to go to the big cabin and join everyone. As he was walking up the road, Emily and Rob ran past him to go feed the dogs down at the little cabin. About five minutes later, they came bursting into the big cabin yelling. "Did you see it? Did you see it?" Everyone said "what?" and they replied. It was the biggest shooting star they had ever seen! They said it was so bright, they saw their shadows on the ground in front of them. When they turned around a green, orange and red fireball roared by in the sky above. John was reminded that God is with him, but works on His time, not ours, and that we need to be patient and adhere to the numerous scripture commands to "wait on the Lord".

Emily recalls it this way, "The ranch is a perfect place for soul searching and exploring who God is. One particular night my brother Rob and I were talking about faith while walking towards Nonnie and Grandad's cabin when all of the sudden it was as if the night around us became day due to a giant shooting star—it lit up the road so much that I remember we could see our shadows. We took it as a sign that God sees us, is with us, and loves us."

* * *

There is an abiding stillness when I am at the ranch. A peace that passes all understanding—a silence in which to dream. The great Comforter—God's Holy Spirit is the atmosphere that surrounds me. The Spring Gap Ranch is a sacred place where I receive comfort and the deepest kind of strength. Many times we will walk the red dirt by the cabin. It is where we still find the old homestead stones and also where Indians camped. We know this because of the arrowheads and shards we have found there.

Jay and I hunted almost a year for arrowheads, mostly in two locations. One close to the little cabin towards "Faircloth's" in the sandy drainage areas. The other was a hillside near a creek between two plateaus in the Sneed pasture. It is tricky to spot the Indian relics and many a scrap of flint has fooled the eye and made the heart jump. Every time we found a complete arrowhead was great joy. It was like a sand dollar on the beach. We mounted the points by stitching them onto a piece of leather, framed that, and presented it to Dad. There is a spiritual practice of naming, of knowing, of remembering that acts like a standing stone, an Ebenezer. This godly heritage is what we pray for our children, and their children, and all the generations.

Eleven

Fluff and Filler

INTRIGUING RUMORS

I will also meditate on all Your work,
And talk of Your deeds.
Psalm 77:12

BURIED TREASURE! What a great lure to get kids hiking and telling stories about what they know and mostly don't know. Pirates, banditos, train robbers—it's all possible. The Western Trail was just a few miles off the ranch. Hundreds of people, cattle, and horses traversed it. Like a dry river bed, it flowed with early life and history. Growing up, Dad told us the secret story of buried treasure on the ranch. It was important to look for three markings on a rock. A coiled snake, a turkey track, and a star. Each of our families has their own version. Emily's includes 16 donkey loads of gold that was hidden on the ranch after a Spanish caravan was ambushed by Indians. Supposedly the gold is still lost somewhere in a sandstone cave on the ranch, potentially at the bottom of a 'bottomless pit', and guarded by a rattlesnake den. What a motherlode that would be. And it's not completely far-fetched. There are several "marked" rocks across the area where people have risked their lives and lost their fortunes chasing after the riches. An example is The Spider Rock Legend which involves coded stone maps. One set of markings discovered near Kiowa Peak, pointed towards locations in Callahan County. These maps are believed to mark the site of a significant, yet still unfound, Spanish treasure. For generations, hunters have excavated sites in the area hoping to find a gold cache, often linked to accounts of Coronado or early Spanish exploration. The Spaniards buried something fantastic in the lonely West Texas terrain, where they were mining precious metals. And people are still looking for it today.

Dad was fairly serious in his belief that hidden treasure was on the ranch. One time, when I was about ten years old, we had taken a picnic to the ranch and were then going to explore a cave that could possibly be "the spot". Dad went in first, then Rob, then me. From behind, Lynn climbed the ledge and came face to face with a rattlesnake with more all along the ledge. Mom said something like "Bob, stop, there are snakes all over the rim." We had gone into a rattlesnake den. We slowly backed out. It must have been a time of year that was still cool and perhaps they weren't moving yet. It was God's hand moving us back. Those buzztails were etched in my brain as a danger I don't forget. After that episode we didn't hunt the treasure anymore. As an adult, Rob has explored several caverns with cameras on scopes. And we all believe that it is possible for the treasure to be on the ranch. As for me and my house, we will continue to embellish and pass on Dad's story.

* * *

The next two vignettes occurred in the 1970's and come from John.

I have mentioned our bulldozer operator, Blanton Childress previously. He was a real character and half crazy. However, you would have to be at least "half a bubble off" to be willing to drive a bulldozer over 10,000 acres for 15 years. He believed that the Earth was flat. When the astronauts landed on the moon in 1969, he said they were sent to the other side of the flat earth and were criminals that were offered their freedom for the dangerous trip to the other side of the flat earth. Another time, he came rushing to the headquarters from the field, telling Dad and Vernon that a bunch of Nazis had landed in a hot air balloon a couple of miles away from where he was running the bulldozer. He said they all jumped out yelling in German that he couldn't understand and that they had machine guns, which they pointed them at him until he got in his pick up and left the bulldozer. Dad and Vernon rode back with him and, of course, found nothing. But you could not convince Blanton that he had not seen what he had seen!

Blanton could also fly off the handle. Dad told me that one time they were working cattle and he was in the pens with the cowboys. Blanton drove up in his pickup to tell Dad about the bulldozer breaking down and a new part needed. Dad waved him off and said he would get with him in a few minutes once he finished what they were doing with the cattle. When Dad walked over to Blanton, he was holding a large socket wrench and told Dad he was going to whup him because he had embarrassed him in front of the cowboys by waving him off. Dad calmly explained to him that they were in the middle of separating cows from calves and he was needed where he was and did not mean disrespect. Dad then told him that if he wanted to fight, he'd give it to him, but reminded Blanton that he was 20 years younger and would probably end up on top. Blanton put the wrench down and everything was back to good.

It is also worth remembering that we used to run Spanish goats – 5000 of them! Dad, as part of his stewardship and desire to clear brush, primarily scrub oak that cropped up after the controlled burns, stocked the ranch with goats and would rotate them from pasture to pasture. The goats were very effective at eating and killing the brush, but the coyotes put us out of the goat business. Since no one else was running goats near us, we became a magnet for coyotes, and hundreds could be heard every night howling. The thing that aggravated Dad the most, was that the coyotes would kill for pleasure, not just to eat. We would come upon killing fields where 150 goats would be dead, but very few eaten. He hired trappers to thin them out, but it was a losing battle. The last year Dad had goats, he lost 1500 out of the 5000.

For many years after we were out of the goat business, a lone Billy goat traveled with the cattle herd. He must have been fairly safe because he lived long enough to become a family legend. We loved the goats and almost every spring Dad would bring an orphaned baby goat into town for us to raise. Lynn has always had an amazing gift with animals. She seems to be able to communicate safety and love. She would spend hours bottle feeding, and would have slept outside with them had my parents let her.

* * *

We always had dogs. Border Collies and bird dogs mark my childhood days. We also had several litters of puppies and learned much about life from those pets. John has carried on with hunting dogs and a Border Terrier. Rob branched out to Labrador Retrievers and a Toy Australian Shepherd. Lynn has a Toy Australian Shepherd, Dachshunds and Pitbulls. And Jay and I have a Toy Australian Shepherd. Our love for animals as companions comes from parents who allowed our home to be filled with pets. Dad would also bring home baby squirrels that had fallen out of their nest and been abandoned. Again they were bottle fed round the clock. We were quite the neighborhood attraction until the squirrels became adults and started biting. Wild things are made for the wild. Learning to let go was never easy but it taught us to appreciate and be grateful.

* * *

My last story involves an animal, but not the kind you might think of on a West Texas ranch. Mom had a sneaky sense of humor. She was highly educated and a very thoughtful person. She didn't care for silliness but appreciated a well thought out surprise. As my parents got older, they had less need for material things. They were not extravagant people. My dad once told me, "Some people like to spend their money on fancy cars and fur coats, but we prefer to travel." And we did.

Their love for fishing led them to a house on Lake Brownwood not far from the ranch. It happened to be close to the State Park and a Putt-Putt golf course. The course was still open when I was younger but not for long. Then like all things unattended, it became overgrown with shrubs and tall weeds. The unique thing about this course was the decorative animal statues for each hole. One of those was a ten foot tall giraffe leaning down pretending to eat. Mom had noticed that the land was for sale so she contacted the owner and procured the giraffe. She had it moved to the Uncle George pasture and awarded it to my dad. He loved it. They once traveled to Africa and I'm sure the giraffe statue in the little blue stem was an imaginative savanna.

Mom had no idea how much fun we would have with that giraffe! The first roundup after it arrived was one where the cowboys still used their horses to gather the cattle. It was quite the rodeo when the horses came trotting over the hill and about the same time the cowboys noticed it so did they. Between checking their eyes and staying in the saddle the words were flying. And I still laugh when I think about the young beau Twig brought home from her art school in New York City. We always take people out to the ranch especially if they are not from Texas. We told this young man to keep his eyes open as we had a runaway giraffe on the ranch and we had not been able to capture it. He was giddy when he spotted it and we asked if maybe we should try and walk up on it. Of course he was game and it took him till we were about ten yards from it to stop and say wait, it's not moving. Gratefully he laughed with us and a steak dinner later sealed our forgiveness.

Our lives are stories built on small moments and the Spring Gap has provided many of them. As we weave them into the tapestry of our times together, our history becomes richer and fuller. We have disagreements and varying opinions like a real family. Thankfully, our parents showed us how to get along. To pray, "O Lord, contain me in Your calmness." That to understand was more important than being right. There have been hard moments, moments that insist we pause and pause some more. And because of this foundational faith that we all share, our ranch has been held together in God's power, not our own.

Twelve

Leaving Legacy

AN ANCIENT SONG

Therefore know that the Lord your God, He is God,
the faithful God who keeps covenant and mercy
for a thousand generations with those
who love Him and keep His commandments.
Deuteronomy 7:9

LIFE CONTINUES AND WILL CONTINUE long after I'm gone. In the poet T.S. Eliot's message from the Four Quartets he says; "We will spend our lives exploring only to find, at the end, we have returned to our beginning, but this time with understanding." The ranch has made us, it's in our DNA. Our clothes carry the stains of sweat and dirt. Our hearts are like cords that once woven together have formed an ancestral bond. We were made to collaborate. When Dad left the ranch to John, Lynn, Rob, and me he did so with few caveats. He hoped we would continue with the cow/calf operation, but it wasn't a "have to". He preferred to keep the land pristine and we have held back the wind turbine business from taking over our landscape. Management wise we use a committee approach having input from the siblings and spouses. Dad suggested that only one of us work with the foreman so John has handled that since Dad passed away. He is passing that baton to Rob and we anticipate starting the ranch's next century with a new foreman, our sixth. It is the work of many hands committed to building daily relationships.

Sacred places need not be perfect, but they cease to be sacred if nobody cares for them. John emphasizes that Dad made it clear to us that we were free to do what we wanted with the ranch, including selling it. This has given us all much freedom and, I think, increased our enjoyment of the ranch. Our children have watched us work together. We give them the same freedom as the years move forward and the ranch is again transferred to the coming generations. Dad poured his heart and energy into the ranch and got wonderful satisfaction from it. And he taught us to choose lives that we enjoy and give satisfaction. He pursued his passion and wasn't afraid to change horses mid-stream. These lessons reflect small daily choices. They express the character and faith beginning with C.M., to Agnes, to Bob and now ours. They are written in the wind, the sunsets, and the shining stars at night. Now the roots of our lives are sunk deep in something ancient and beloved.

Nature inspires creativity. They are intrinsically connected and expressed through many mediums. The Spring Gap Ranch has been the subject of many painters and photographers. Twig Capra, Emily Beckham Wood, and myself collaborated on an art show at the Cockerell Fine Art Gallery drawing honor to the ranch. Emily and myself, as painters, and Twig, as a photographer. We used our deep love of the Spring Gap to emphasize our favorite moments. A shared goal was capturing the tangible miracles around the everyday ordinary. This collection expressed the joy of the simple ranch life. Emily painted some of her cowboy mentors and gave those paintings as gifts to Arlon Baize and Sammy Cochran. Legacy has many forms and that is what we hope to leave for our children and their children unto however many generations would like to keep something so mysterious and precious. Every generation will look like what it is: one more beginning and one more step towards new ideas. They will make a way in the place God calls them. Our "trail" of stories leaves behind an enduring mark to chronicle the changes and contributions we made. It is a campfire they can sit around and percolate their own ideas and visions. We never choose the day our dream will come true. But we all dream of the rest and peace we imagine waits for us at the end of a long journey. The ranch has poured out blessings in the natural and in the spiritual. We have received a love of nature, love of God's creation, desire for solitude and listening to the still quiet voice, joy in stargazing, treasured time with family, ability to relate to and enjoy people of different backgrounds, appreciation for weather, and so much more. Nature makes no demands of us save only that of being aware.

As we close this 100 years, it seems fitting to share a thought from Mom, "Happy is the one who loves the little things of life. Laughter, silence, dewdrops, toadstools, small truths. If we could only see---the horizon that stays our sight is but the gateway to God's greater plan." I'll end with the next generation's thoughts and an anecdote from Twig Capra. May the Lord bless and keep us all. May He make His face shine upon us. May He be gracious to us and give us peace.

I think of the joy of family time uninterrupted. I think of the wonder of my own kids at a place they can wander with no one watching. The world is uncertain and sometimes I fear for their future, but in this place, I am able to feel Nonnie's presence telling me that all shall be well, and all shall be well, and all manner of things shall be well.

—Michael Beckham

There is a stillness you cannot find in the city. It is a place where fresh air takes the night sky, and reveals more stars than I have ever seen. A true place of stillness and serenity> The Spring Gap Ranch is more than just a place filled with memories. It is part of our life and my heart that brings peace to my soul.

—Justin Marderosian

As a kid, it was just part of life. Looking back, it taught me responsibility, patience, and how to work without needing recognition. The ranch showed me that things worth having take time, and that showing up matters. Those lessons stayed with me long after I stopped going out there every weekend.

—Austin Beckham

Walking up to Nonnie and Grandad's cabin from the bigger family cabin was always a fun little adventure. Nonnie would often come down to help me look for frogs or tadpoles at the pond bringing a jar from their cabin, or find me up in a large tree right by their cabin. Those memories with Nonnie, and the warmth I still feel in them, are forever cherished in my mind.

—Emily Beckham

Later on, in college, I started going back with friends. We'd ride through the pastures, talk for hours, and on hot days jump into the tanks to cool off. It felt different than it did when I was younger, but in a good way—less about games and more about being together. Going back reminded me how special it was to have one place tied to so many stages of life. Spring Gap Ranch holds some of my simplest and best memories, and it's a place I'll always associate with friendship, freedom, and growing up.

—Alex Beckham

* * *

The mirror that nature holds is deep and floating and ethereal and faithful. A clean bright mirror, a magical wondrous mirror, it will show you all you can conceive of; all you wish to behold. That is unless you're driving across the pasture as your rearview shows nothing but plumes of white caliche kicked up in your tracks. Somewhere past the dust cloud is the seamless horizon line that abides in the heat and wind of West Texas. In time, the rain will come to settle the score and exposed bone will be replaced by blood red clay as the scent of iron and juniper spread across the plains. This land follows close upon the mood of the mind that reads it and reflects: is harsh as it is harsh, bright as it is bright, laughs in its laughter, weeps in its tears. Nonnie's taste for poetry definitively set the tone for my appreciation of the ranch and the repercussions such a wide open space for reflection has ultimately had on my worldview. Her collection of Whitman and Blake were seminal texts that led me down a path through my own wilderness, and if not for their dog-eared maps I might still be lost. The ranch played backdrop for a childhood spent reliving the tales of Robin Hood and Middle Earth and the land that once belonged to Comanche did not despair over our imaginary histories but simply stood watch as we grew like weeds amongst their fossil foothills. Through drought or flood, grandiose migrations or humble fawn births-nature continued to reflect our multitudes.

> "To go forth now from all the entanglement
> that is ours and yet not ours, that,
> like the water in an old well, reflects us in fragments,
> distorts what we are.
> From all that clings like burrs and brambles
> —to go forth and see for once,
> close up, afresh, what we had ceased to see
> —so familiar it had become."
> -Rainer Maria Rilke,
> from The Departure of the Prodigal Son

When the reflection in the well grew unfamiliar, for a time the ranch didn't feel so welcoming to me. I only saw it for its empty spaces and rough edges. The cowboys gave me guff, and even Grandad took great convincing to remember my name (he is forgiven for his final forgetting.) In her way, Nonnie always knew. An Episcopalian, her openness to diverse interpretation over dogma had marked her a kindred spirit to my own and helped foster a perspective that saw value in both the blossoms and the briars. Her love remains rooted in my memory like a Mesquite-resilient, tough, and sweet. Empathy that defied erosion in the face of life's many wildfires was a hard earned quality that her many annotated, well-worn books can attest came from years of continued reflection and adaptation. The parts of her library that we each carried into our own lives were like seed pods scattered in the wind.

Later in life while making art in New York City, I was given advice after a portfolio review 'to always leave a little Texas mud on my boots'. At the time I didn't think too much of the idea, but now I cherish the thought. Red dirt will always be on my boots, straight from the Spring Gap. One day when nature eventually turns its mirror to reflect on me, I hope it is in the sight of a West Texas sunset. —Twig Capra

SPRING GAP RANCH

I would like to express my sincere gratitude to the Maker of this wild, beautiful world. I am particularly grateful to Him for giving me a place to belong and share. God is the Word that made the world, the source of all goodness, glory, and truth. I thank Him for guiding me to write and tell His story.

I completed this project with Jay, my creative and thoughtful husband, who brought me cool water while I walked in the memories of our family. I dreamed it, he supported it, and together we conceived a legacy. His continual editing and oversight has made this a better read. Jay, I love you and I love the life we enjoy together.

To all the Spring Gap family, thank you for the gifts of remembering and photography. Your portraits and snapshots have become precious heirlooms. Your stories have given me new insight and deep belly laughs. How blessed we are to be knitted together in this tapestry called family. Our prayer for all the younger generations is that you find ways to come together and be interested in each other. The vast array of talents and gifts represented in yourselves and your children is abundantly rich.

A deep and wide range of appreciation to the Baize family. Arlon and Paige watched over us, and we never had a mishap with their faithful care. Paige was the first to immortalize the ranch in his book, Remembering, and I am grateful he did. The description of roundup rings truer because of his insights. Arlon always brought heart and faith to our gatherings, and his prayers kept us focused on the main thing regardless of how our day was going.

Special thanks to my Master Mind group, Kim Dobbs, Kimberly Nihart, and Karen Vickers. Thank you for praying with me and giving me the gift of fruitful conversations. Your consistently solid advice was given generously and at just the right moments. Thanks to Patricia Day, Kim Dobbs, David Romanik, Tamara Trail, Vicki Tuegel, and Nancy Weaver for their wonderful feedback on an early draft. And to Sally Capra a special thanks for her amazing editing skills. Her commas helped organize my thoughts and gave good form to the manuscript.

I cannot count the number of times I thank our Lord for all of you, for your faithfulness and generosity to pray for me. For the honor it has been to work with you all. This story is proof that well-loved places can be havens for producing, belonging, healing and rest. As we move into the coming years, the Spring Gap Ranch will continue to carry light and joy. It flows in springs of living water. Soli Deo Gloria.

Nancy Beckham Capra graduated from the University of Texas in Austin with a BA in Drama. She teaches painting and creativity to children and women through Willow Art School.

Nancy is intrigued by the idea of color, light and movement combined with the power and authority of God. By blending these elements of beauty and truth she creates faith-based art. She continues seeking God's voice and wisdom along with training her eye as lifelong pursuits. Her writing provides an opportunity to connect with others and leave a tangible expression of how God moves. Combining writing and art is providing a door to a larger audience to encourage healing through art coaching.

Nancy is married to Jay and has three adult children, and five grandchildren. Creating paintings and writing stories allows Nancy to walk in her God-designed destiny.